The Recovery
of the
Teaching Ministry

J. STANLEY GLEN

The
Recovery
of the
Teaching
Ministry

THE
WESTMINSTER
PRESS

Philadelphia

Contents

⇔ | Foreword

This study began as a practical problem. It soon broadened to include much that was not originally anticipated and that for the most part could have been pursued indefinitely. It revealed itself as one of those problems which grow larger and larger the more one works at them until a point is reached where one has to decide somewhat arbitrarily to bring them to an end. This alternative seemed preferable chiefly for the purpose of sharing the material with others who may be sensitive to the same problem. In so far, therefore, as the study promotes discussion and stimulates investigation the writer would beg the indulgence of the reader for its limitations. To some extent these have been due to the toll that administrative duties take of time and strength. Nevertheless, these duties helped to focus the problem and to lay it as much upon the heart as upon the mind.

When, in the midst of such an undertaking, the invitation arrived from Columbia Theological Seminary, Decatur, Georgia, to become the Smyth lecturer for November, 1959, it seemed only natural to adopt it as the subject. The preparation for these lectures as well as the fellowship with the faculty and students was a most gratifying experience. Appreciation is due especially to President J. McDowell Richards for his great kindness and to those of his colleagues who shared in extending the

7

hospitality of the seminary to me. The last two lectures of the five delivered have been revised substantially for publication, and a sixth has been added to indicate some of the more important conclusions. The order also has been changed. Chapters one, three, four, and parts of two and five represent what was attempted at Columbia.

This foreword would not be complete without an expression of gratitude to my wife, Winifred, who has had a lively interest in the subject from the beginning. Her insight and helpful suggestions have contributed much to the whole study.

J. S. G.

Knox College
Toronto, Canada

1 | The Subordination of the Teaching Ministry

1. *Introduction*

In spite of the traditional emphasis that the church has placed on catechetical instruction and the education of its ministry, as well as the emphasis it has placed on its Sunday schools and the movement represented by them, a strange subordination of the teaching function pervades its life, work, worship, and proclamation. The subordination is not a surface phenomenon due only to limitations at the administrative level, but a spiritual phenomenon due to a deeper, underlying condition, which robs the teaching ministry of its power and obstructs it in relation to the constitutive source of faith.

The existence of such a phenomenon is difficult to explain, especially at a time when public education is so widely recognized and developed. One would have expected that the sheer competition of ideas and the counterclaims of menacing ideologies would have stimulated the church to develop its teaching ministry to an unparalleled degree. But this has not been the case. The subordination stubbornly persists. Not even the large and important place that the task of teaching had in the ministry of Jesus, nor the obvious place that it had in Judaism, have had much effect upon it. A strange resistance, even from the most unexpected quarters, makes the teaching ministry harder to develop than any other.

9

The problem only becomes apparent in a gradual and cumulative manner after an analysis of certain somewhat obvious features of church life and work which are usually taken for granted as integral to common practice. Concealed as it is under the obvious and the commonplace, it attracts little attention and less, if any, curiosity. But when explored in all its ramifications and examined at its point of origin, it emerges as a problem of major proportions. As such it is probably more indicative of the ethos of conventional Christianity than many of the official statements of doctrine which seldom even hint of the subordination.

2. *The Contrast Between the Sanctuary and the Classroom*

The most obvious feature with which to begin is the contrast that obtains in many churches between the sanctuary and the classroom. The scene may be that of any average church of modest means with a conventional pattern of religious life. Let an unbiased observer casually stroll through such a church to see where its main interest lies. Let him stroll through the sanctuary, then through the classroom, and then ask himself what his impressions are. He will reply that everything suggests an almost exclusive devotion to the sanctuary, accompanied by an indifference to the classroom which in many instances is little short of contempt. The contrast will be most evident in the furnishings and equipment, which, in its own way, is a sobering parable to those able to discern its ultimate significance. In the sanctuary, with its frequent cathedral-like pre-eminence, will be found the most expensive altars, Communion tables, pulpits, organs, stained-glass windows, pews, and carpets, often embodying the most exquisite resources of architecture and art. But in the classroom, in sharpest contrast to the finery of the sanctuary, it seems that almost anything will do. Even the most essential equipment, which in a secular classroom will seldom if ever be lacking, is not to be found here. Maps and blackboards and adequate library facilities are almost nonexistent. Even though the public library is an accepted institution in modern society, and the number of helpful books on every aspect of the Christian faith has never been so great, a congregational library is lacking; and, typically, the classroom is relegated to a basement or back room as if to accentuate its subordinate role.

The contrast is too sharp to be removed by the simple expedient of providing new buildings and equipment, because it extends to the quality of personnel and to the spirit that pervades the sanctuary and the classroom and determines the manner in which each conceives of its task. For the reverence and the solemnity of the one is too frequently contradicted by the irreverence and the triviality of the other, as though the one mainly existed for the purpose of undoing the work of the other. There is no doubt that new buildings and equipment are often indicative of an enlarged interest in the classroom, but they may also betray the fact that the classroom is still subordinated — not, of course, in the way it previously was when it was poor and neglected, but in a prosperous way. A great diversity of activity will now conceal the fact that there is so little for the mind. There will be something, of course, for everyone, for all age groups, for those with special interests and with special problems, but little to confront any of them with the intelligible content of the Christian faith. Not that one should discount the importance of such activities if they provide wholesome recreation and the nearest thing to the atmosphere of a home. But why the subordination of the ministry to the mind? Why the expensive kitchens, assembly halls, lounges, carpets, and drapes, and still no maps, blackboards, and books? Why so much attention to games and still no teacher training?

There is a danger, of course, in drawing too sharp a distinction between the classroom and the sanctuary, because the latter has its own peculiar educative function, which at best may be described as the wisdom that comes of the fear of the Lord. When such wisdom abounds it can scarcely be said that the teaching ministry has been subordinated, because such wisdom is the root of all subsequent religious instruction. In it we find the anterior factor which prevents the instruction from becoming facile, and as a result from becoming irrelevant. In this sense the wisdom found in the sanctuary has an intelligibility which is anterior to that of instruction. But the point one wishes to make is that the subordination of the teaching ministry pertains as much to the sanctuary as it does to the classroom, because if the sanctuary subordinates the classroom it is only because the sanctuary has already subordinated within itself the wisdom which is the root of all that the classroom does. Having failed to begin with the fear of the Lord, it has not learned the wisdom of the Lord.

But how is this possible? In what way does the sanctuary subordinate the wisdom that properly belongs to it? If a brief answer may be permitted, one would have to reply that it does it chiefly by means of a form of holiness that permits the worshiper to rise above the intelligible into the ineffable. It is a holiness devoid of responsibility for truth. The reason such holiness appeals to the worshiper is probably because it affords him an escape from thinking — particularly the thinking from the heart, which is an appropriate response to the wisdom of God. Since all thinking of such a nature involves a degree of suffering, the worshiper recoils from it and expects instead that the chief function of the holy is to inspire him, with no prior consciousness of the fearful thing it is to fall into the hands of the living God (Heb. 10:31). Such worship may be very well described as worship, but not as Christian worship.

There is a similar danger of drawing too sharp a distinction between the classroom and the pulpit as though the latter were not also a place of instruction. The classroom must in no sense rob the pulpit of its teaching function, nor cast any doubt on the excellence of its opportunity in the presence of a waiting congregation. For the pulpit tradition inherited from the Protestant Reformation, and indirectly from the Jewish synagogue, demands that the pulpit assume a major responsibility for teaching. But the unfortunate fact which overshadows such a possibility is the persistent subordination of the teaching function of the pulpit itself.

What this means will be seen in the fact that the pulpit frequently disregards the most elementary principles of the learning process, and in this way the humanity of the hearer. An examination of published sermons will often reveal how little didactic content they possess. The structure, from a pedagogical point of view, is often obscure, and the terminology seldom clarified. The meaning of the sacred vocabulary is assumed as self-evident to the average listener. Usually a tremendous leap is made from the Biblical era to the present age, as though the intervening centuries did not matter. In the practical planning of the pulpit program, the selection of sermons is usually at random from any part of the Bible, except for the occasional series. The resulting fragmentation of the wholeness of the Biblical books and passages adds its own measure of confusion. The mode of communication is restricted to a unilateral relationship in which the silent congregation is a serious obstacle to the teaching function. The people are never given an opportunity of asking questions. The preacher therefore frequently fails to make an effective contact with their world and remains separated in his world from theirs. It is not difficult, therefore, to understand why so many otherwise gifted and capable Christians grasp so little of the intelligible content of the faith they profess, even after hearing hundreds of sermons over the years. It derives from the fact that the task of homiletics is so largely divorced from Christian education.

An objection will be raised, of course, that one dare not let down the bars and transform the service of preaching into a popular forum or a question-and-answer period. It will be said that the preacher delivering his message to a silent congregation symbolizes the peculiar authority of his calling. He must speak and they must listen. But to this objection, and without countenancing any cheapened substitute, it may be said that the type of communication most frequently used by Christ was not the formal sermon but pastoral conversation. Even when he preached in the synagogues, not to say anything of seaside, plain, and mountain, the people could always ask their questions. Neither he nor his disciples required the protection of a pulpit, or the convenience of a silent congregation, as a symbolical manifestation of their unique authority. Nor did any of the prophets before them require such an arrangement before they could utter with evident certainty, " Thus saith the Lord."

3. *The Optional Nature of the Minister's Teaching Role*

If now we are prepared to recognize that the subordination of the teaching ministry pertains not only to the classroom but to the pulpit, we should proceed to recognize that it pertains to our total conception of the ministry itself. This will mean a recognition of how the teaching ministry is subordinated in the various roles a minister is expected to play in the practical work of his congregation. In the first place, the fact of subordination is conspicuous in the optional nature of his teaching role in comparison with other roles. He may choose to teach or not to teach. If he does not teach, no one will call him into question. If he does teach, his action may even be regarded as exceptional. But he has no such liberty of choice in respect to other roles. He must conduct public worship. He must preach. He must provide the sacraments. He must engage in pastoral work. He must devote himself to church organization. All of these are compulsory in a way in which the teaching role is not. If he neglects them, he will involve himself in difficulties with his people and the ecclesiastical authorities to whom he is subject.

The extent to which this difference enters into the life and work of the church may be seen in the way in which the congregation normally conceives of the various roles expected of a minister. They will readily think of him as the preacher who appears at stated intervals in the pulpit, as the celebrant of the sacraments who baptizes and gives Holy Communion, as the pastor who counsels those in trouble, as the administrator of the organizational life and structure of the congregation whose duty it is to direct its affairs and facilitate its programs. But they will seldom think of him as *the* teacher. Even in those churches where the practice of catechizing the children once earned him recognition as the teacher in a restricted sense, the practice has largely declined, if it has not disappeared. If he is regarded as the teaching elder, it is almost entirely a theoretical distinction at the ecclesiastical level and not one that is proven by professional training and by experience in the classroom, and not one that is familiar to the people.

These observations on the optional nature of the minister's teaching role are confirmed by recent sociological studies [1] which have shown how limited and unimportant it is in the average ministry. The time devoted to it in the minister's working day is only the merest fraction of the time devoted to his other roles. What is even more surprising is the low rating that ministers give to intelligence as a factor in success, and the equally low rating they give it in achieving an effective ministry apart from success.

All in all, it is evident from sociological studies that the world of ideas presupposed by any teaching ministry is accorded less of a place in the life and work of the church than it is often presumed to have. To put it plainly, the minister's ability to win friends and influence people is of greater importance to him than his ability to read, study, and think. A business office is more representative of his actual roles than a study filled with the best books and papers.

But this situation is not inevitable. There is no valid reason why the teaching role should not be as compulsory for the minister as any other role. There is no valid reason why he should not be required to teach with the same regularity as he performs his other tasks. One of the best illustrations of this possibility is the role of the rabbi in Judaism, whose primary task has always been regarded as that of teaching. This tradition was carried forward not only into the ministry of Jesus, whose teaching role was so conspicuous, but into the ministry of the apostles, as we see from the practice of Paul, who frequently availed himself of the teaching privileges of the synagogue.

But in calling attention to such a possibility it should not be inferred that the only alternative is that of expecting the minister to do all the teaching. In some instances this would be possible and desirable, but in most instances it would be impractical because of the size of the task. What is being stressed is that he be recognized as *the* teacher as he is *the* preacher and *the* pastor, and this not merely in a theoretical sense but as proven by professional training and experience in the classroom. This should be evident above all in the pulpit, which has suffered so long from an unjustifiable separation of homiletics from Christian education.[2] Outside the pulpit it should be evident in his ability to become a teacher of teachers and of new communicants and of those who come with the deepest and most complex problems of life and thought, and in every case not with a sporadic, seasonal effort of a few weeks duration, but with a continuous effort over the year, which is as compulsory as his preaching. This, more than anything else, would assist in solving the perennial problem of finding competent teachers for the Sunday school and competent leadership for the whole life and work of the church.

The question inevitably raised by such insistence upon the compulsory nature of the minister's teaching role is whether this is expecting too much in view of the New Testament assertion that among Christ's gifts to the church some should be apostles, some evangelists, some pastors and teachers (Eph. 4:11). It will be asked whether we can expect every minister to be a teacher when the New Testament does not expect it. The question, to be more specific, is whether we have a right to expect that evangelists and pastors be teachers. The answer to these questions necessitates a distinction being drawn between teaching as a special gift and therefore as a specialized field of service, and teaching as a function which is integral to everything that the ministry involves. In this latter sense, it is anything but an optional function. What we have to recognize is that the subordination of the teaching ministry is not merely the subordination of a few men with special gifts but the subordination of a function which properly belongs to every ministry and to the entire witness, worship, life, and work of the church. It is the subordination of the intelligible content of the Christian faith, without which worship is not worship, preaching is not preaching, and pastoral work not pastoral.

But if this is the case, why has the church permitted the subordination of the intelligible content of the faith when such content is equivalent to the truth of the faith? Are we to understand from this that the optional nature of the minister's teaching role is tantamount to an optional attitude to the truth? Are we to understand that the congregation that condones his liberty in this respect is unwittingly acknowledging that it does not expect him to be responsible for the truth? Whatever be the answer to such questions, the significant fact that emerges is that the minister's teaching role does not possess the same status as his preaching, pastoral, and sacramental roles. It does not even possess the same status as his administrative role. The surprising thing, moreover, is that it does not possess the power of maintaining its status in competition with these roles, as we see from the ease with which it is surrendered to the unqualified Sunday school teacher. The ministry of the Word and sacraments would never be surrendered with the same facility.

Further evidence of the lower status of the teaching role may be seen in a comparison of the educational qualifications of the average Sunday school teacher with those of the minister of the Word and sacraments, in the case of the former extremely limited, in the case of the latter six or seven years of higher education followed by ordination. The question this naturally suggests is whether the teaching ministry of the church is so unimportant that such a disparity is permitted.[3] The fact that the disparity is so widely accepted as part of the practical tradition of the church leads one to believe that its roots are deep and extensive, reaching down into the substratum of its life and back a long way into its history. What accentuates this suspicion is the fact that we ordain ministers but do not ordain Sunday school teachers. The reason for this difference of practice is not adequately explained by the degree of importance we may attach to the former in comparison to the latter, because the task of the Sunday school is of the greatest significance in the ongoing life of the church. The more probable explanation is that ministers are ordained because their task possesses charismatic significance while that of the Sunday school teacher does not possess it. That is to say, the Sunday school teacher is not regarded as one who is called of God for his task. He is what is known as a voluntary worker which, in view of our analysis, means more than the fact that he volunteers his services. It means rather that he, like the minister, conceives of his teaching role as optional.

These observations suggest that the primary reason for the subordination of the teaching ministry is a false separation of grace from truth. Grace is regarded as charismatic and in principle devoid of truth, while truth is regarded as noncharismatic and in principle devoid of grace. Since it is the teaching ministry that is responsible for the truth, this means that the teaching ministry is subordinated *ipso facto* if truth is not charismatic. If we wish, moreover, to know why the teaching ministry does not even possess the status of church administration, it is probably because church administration involves a secular equivalent of grace. Administration is in essence a matter of personal relationship for which the mystery of the right personality is efficacious. Its secret is to be found in graciousness, which is nothing other than a secularized form of grace in which personal charm, impressiveness, and popularity are the superficial equivalents of charismatic power. In this sense the graciousness of man is substituted for the grace of God, and in its own way subordinates the teaching ministry. Church administration for this reason takes precedence over teaching.

4. *The Form of the Problem in Theological Education*

Although the subordination of the teaching ministry is less obvious in theological education than it is elsewhere, it is just as real and as serious and, if anything, more complex. Even if it must be said of such education that it is the area in which the most thorough teaching effort of the church is to be found, this ought not to deceive us into believing that the problem is here less acute. Nor should the surface manifestations of the problem, particularly in the field of practical theology, detract our attention from its deeper and more complex expression in the traditional theological subjects and within these subjects, particularly in the manner in which the interpretation of Scripture is conceived.

In a preliminary way, of course, it is not difficult to identify these surface manifestations in the practical field. For one thing, we are certain that ministers are not trained as teachers because theological education makes little or no provision for it. Instead of recognizing the way in which the cognate functions of teaching and learning enter into everything a minister does and characterize the human side of his work, theological education restricts its conception of these functions to the narrowly specialized task of teaching as a specific calling. While it is true that an increasing number of theological schools are providing courses in Christian education, these are often electives rather than required subjects, and seldom if ever the kind of practice-teaching in the classroom in which the student acquires a firsthand knowledge of his power and limitation as a teacher and of the complexities of the learning process. To some extent this neglect of training in practical pedagogy may be due to the bias of university education against it which has carried over into theological education, but it is also due to the implicit assumption of Biblicism that a knowledge of the Bible is sufficient without it. A deeply rooted assumption persists that practical pedagogy is only for the specialist and, if anything, a matter intended for children.

Closely related to the neglect of practical pedagogy is the neglect of practical homiletics. For in most if not all theological seminaries the relatively small number of sermons that are actually delivered by a student under careful supervision as a requirement for graduation is patently absurd. In no other comparable vocation would such limited training in one of its principal tasks be permitted. Reputable teachers' colleges do not send their graduates out into the high schools and grammar schools with as limited a preliminary training in practice-teaching. Nor do medical schools permit their students to graduate with as limited a practical training in any task as important to the profession as preaching is to the ministry. Objections may be raised, of course, that a simple comparison at this level between the theological seminary and the teachers' college or the medical school is scarcely valid, and furthermore that an already overloaded curriculum would forbid the addition of practical pedagogy or of more practical homiletics. In assessing such objections, let it be said that we are not concerned at the moment with arguing them point by point. Nor are we concerned with a merely pragmatic solution. For whatever may be said against our comparison, the disparity that it reveals is too great to be explained away by any appeal to matters of detail.

What we have said of the neglect of practical homiletics is related, however, to another surface manifestation of the subordination of the teaching ministry. This has to do with the divorce between homiletics and Christian education. In most theological seminaries the conception of what is involved in the preparation and delivery of sermons has been separated off from the idea of teaching. Both the content and the mode of presentation are considered without any appreciable regard for the function of human learning as an integral aspect of listening to a sermon. The emphasis is almost exclusively on literary and rhetorical considerations, including the cultivation of good manners and speech, with little attention to the problem of how the parishioner hears the sermon and the conditions that obstruct or facilitate his understanding of it, a large proportion of which belong to the field of Christian education.

It ought not be supposed, however, that the subordination of the teaching ministry in the theological seminary is of such a nature that it can be solved by a strong emphasis on practical training, important and beneficial as this may be. At best it would only be a partial solution and would leave untouched the deeper form of the problem implicit in the traditional theological curriculum itself. The fact which at this stage is most significant is the division of the curriculum into two principal parts, which, for the sake of convenience, may be called the theoretical and the practical. On the one hand we have such subjects as Old and New Testament, church history, systematic theology, and apologetics; on the other hand, homiletics, liturgics, pastoral theology, and Christian education. The division is quite familiar and everyone seems to accept it. But it is more than a division within a curriculum. It is a division that reflects a dilemma regarding the nature of truth. For what we find in the case of the theoretical subjects is that the emphasis is laid almost exclusively on the recognition of truth, while in the case of the practical subjects it is laid almost exclusively on the communication of truth. A cleavage exists between the recognition of truth and the communication of truth. As such it represents a far-reaching dilemma within theological education itself, with the scholars on the one side intent upon the discovery of truth and the practicing clergy on the other intent upon the communication of truth. In the one case content tends to be emphasized without regard to communication, in the other communication without regard to content. One may take whole courses in Old and New Testament, for example, with little or no indication that the basic purpose (*raison d'être*) of their content is that of communication. The content will be strictly treated as an end in itself, with the responsibility of its communication left to others. In a comparable way one may take whole courses in homiletics and Christian education with little or no consideration of the basic content of the Bible, including Biblical theology. Communication will be treated as an end in itself, with an emphasis on method divorced from content.

The problem that emerges is the peculiar way in which the communication of truth is subordinated to the recognition of truth. The scholars tend to hold that a thorough knowledge of content is enough to guarantee its communication, with little regard for method. They believe that a student who is thoroughly grounded in the traditional subjects will be largely able to solve the problem of communication with only a limited attention to it as a special field of training. But the practicing clergy on the other hand are impatient of such an assumption, because they have taken too many courses in the seminary in which it has not been substantiated in practice. They have too often thrown their college notes away as having little relevance to the serious nature of their task. They have also had the sobering experience of finding how complex the problem of communication often is at the everyday level where it is obstructed by the limitations of the learning process, by the subtleties of neurotic tendencies, and by the blindness and obstinacy of sin. The result is that a rather persistent conflict obtains between the scholars and the practicing clergy, especially if the latter take the problem of communication seriously. In so far as this conflict influences the theological student and is not resolved it is likely to be productive of two types of graduate — young scholars who are not at heart inclined to the ministry and young ministers who are not at heart inclined to scholarship. In the one case scholarship may even become a means of escape from the ministry, in the other case, an obstacle to be surmounted and left behind in order to begin what is thought to be the real work of the ministry.

In the light of these observations it is legitimate to ask whether the recognition of truth can be separated from the communication of truth without militating against the truth. In other words, is there an adequate recognition of truth without an equally serious acceptance of responsibility for its communication? Is a scholar really a scholar who is not at the same time a teacher? Conversely, is a teacher really a teacher who is not at the same time a scholar? In the last analysis, can our knowledge of truth be separated off from our social responsibility for it? If we wish an illustration, we need only recall how deeply aware many of our modern scientists have become of their social responsibility for the possession of expert knowledge of nuclear energy. On the whole they are less inclined than formerly to divorce such responsibility from the recognition and possession of truth. But what they have experienced of the integral relationship between these two aspects of their task applies in a greater measure than we realize to all truth, and in a special sense to Biblical truth. For although Biblical truth comes to us in pictorial, factual, and propositional form, it is essentially personal in its connotation, having a closer kinship with truth as integrity than with truth as abstraction, as we see for example in Jesus' statement, " I am . . . the truth." Implicit in the knowledge of this kind of truth is an interpersonal relationship which involves social responsibility for it, as may be confirmed by the meaning of the two remaining facets of Jesus' statement, " I am the way . . . and the life " (John 14:6).[4]

What we mean by social responsibility for truth has to do with a sensitivity to the full range and content of it on the part of a scholar, particularly in a discernment of what it does to people when it is communicated to them and they act upon it and embody it in their institutions and in their lives. If an appeal may be made to a familiar illustration, it is like the curator of fossils in a museum who is confronted by the possibility that his particular fossils are always coming alive, acquiring flesh and blood, and walking out of the classroom and out of the notebooks to shape the destiny of men and nations in ways that utterly surprise him. A scholar who is not sensitive to what his fossils become when they assume the proportions of flesh and blood does not really know the truth which he has presumed to recognize. The reason for this is that he has failed to become a teacher.

5. Religious Experience at the Expense of Truth

If we now ask what may be inferred from our discussion and set down as a conclusion to which all the evidence points, we shall have to say that the church is less concerned about the intelligible content of its faith than with the noumenal and the subjective. Instead of holding the two together in a kind of balanced and integral relationship, it tends rather strongly to emphasize the latter at the expense of the former. What this means in plain language is that the church is more interested in religious experience of all kinds, including ecstatic wonder, aesthetic and liturgical impressiveness, sacramental mystery, conversionism, psychologism, the emotional satisfaction of moral achievement, and even the more profane thrill of institutional success than it is with the communication of the intelligible content of its faith, which is mainly represented by the substance of the Bible. By the identification of grace with religious experience it attempts to separate grace off from the truth content of its message. Grace is presumed to be communicable apart from truth, and truth is thereby subordinated.[5]

A little reflection upon this statement will indicate what is meant. The teaching ministry is the one ministry which when taken seriously assumes the responsibility of communicating the truth at the human level and in human form. It insists that the substance of the Bible and of its faith, including the substance of the great confessions of the church, are essentially intelligible and must be communicated from one generation to another if the church is to be the church and men and women are to hear the word of God. This means that the teaching ministry is the guardian of what may be regarded in the best sense as the tradition of the church.

The evidence indicates, however, that the church is less concerned for this than it is for the noumenal and the subjective. Worship is exalted at the expense of preaching, the holy at the expense of the intelligible. Sermons are designed more for the feelings than for the mind. Whether they aim to elicit the conversion experience, exploit the psychological dimensions of personal life, bring comfort, encouragement, and inspiration, or merely to make a good impression, their obvious subjectivity is at the same time a failure to provide instruction. Those who are best qualified to communicate the truth either regard the task as optional or neglect their responsibility. The result is that a spiritual situation gradually develops in which the church has little more to communicate than that which every man may potentially discover for himself.[6]

2 | The Offense of the Teaching Ministry

1. *The Preference for Religious Experience*

Our discussion has led to the conclusion that religious experience is of greater interest to the church than the intelligible content of its faith. Such a conclusion naturally prompts an inquiry into the reasons for the preference and particularly its deeper significance with respect to the teaching ministry. In attempting this inquiry we are not interested in providing an interpretation of the teaching ministry that will be complete in every respect or in providing a general interpretation of the nature of religion. Both are wider problems which require a more extensive treatment. Our only concern is to understand this strange preference for a form of religious experience that is so characterized by its lack of Biblical content as may be generally described as vacuous. Such vacuity pertains not only to information and doctrine, but to that insight and wisdom which come of wrestling with the meaning of the Biblical material, of reflecting upon it and praying over it until it becomes, as it were, that truth in the inward parts of which the psalmist speaks. Nor is such religion entirely lacking in content. For what appears to happen is that the assimilation of Biblical material occurs up to a point beyond which the phenomenon of subordination puts an end to assimilation — which suggests a tension between such religion and the ultimate significance of the Bible.

We begin with the strange ambivalence of the church with respect to the Bible — on the one hand affirmed as divinely inspired, on the other hand allowed to be virtually closed. For if it be divinely inspired, we would naturally expect it to be sought after, entered into, thought through, and listened to with all the earnestness of the man in the parable who sold everything he had to purchase the field in which the treasure was hidden. But it is so frequently neglected despite the number of volumes sold or given away and the schools and pulpits expounding its meaning that we can speak legitimately of the mystery of the closed Bible within the church.

It is always tempting, of course, to argue with considerable effect and with no small measure of truth that the closed Bible is the result of certain contingent factors pertaining to the historical circumstances of its origin and transmission. The Bible, for example, is a large book which in comparison with other books is a formidable volume. It is a complicated book, as the uninitiated reader soon discovers as he tries to thread his way through its intricacies without assistance. It is an ancient book, with a great gulf of history separating its world from that of the present, and what is more, it is a profound book which contrary to popular opinion is more appropriate for adults than for children, and for mature adults at that. But while these factors are important, they are not in principle the root of the problem because they are not insurmountable when one is of a mind to learn from the Bible. There are many large, complicated, profound, and even ancient sources of knowledge that a surprising number of Christians master, not to speak of their frequent expert knowledge in the field of science and technical achievement.

2. *The Question of Irrelevance*

One of the most frequent explanations of the mystery of the closed Bible, especially since Bultmann's controversial proposal,[7] is that the modern man regards its ancient, supernatural perspective as irrelevant. Kraemer, in his *Communication of the Christian Faith,* puts it plainly: " There is a widespread feeling," he says, " that reading the Bible cannot anyhow be a profitable affair. . . . There is, particularly among the lay members of the church, a feeling of helplessness in regard to the Bible. They, of course, have a vague attitude of reverence for the Book, but don't know what to do with it." He concludes that " we must recognize the unintelligibility of the Bible, not only in its language, its terminology, but also, to use a German word, its *Weltbild* (picture of the world). This affects people as antiquated, archaic, unscientific." [8]

While this clear and emphatic statement should leave no doubt of the seriousness of the problem, the attitude of which Kraemer speaks is not so easily explained by the irrelevance of the Biblical perspective as may be thought. The reason for taking exception to such a widely accepted and valid explanation is based upon the recognition that the teaching ministry, however poorly conceived and executed it may be, is nevertheless by comparison with other ministries the one whose aim is to make the Bible more intelligible. It is this ministry, devoted as it is to the increase of relevance and which ought therefore to be doubly welcomed, that is subordinated. Why should this be? If the problem is largely that of irrelevance, why should the ministry which seeks to overcome the irrelevance be resisted?

This suggests that the offense of the Bible is a more important factor in explaining why it is a closed book than current arguments about its irrelevance would indicate. It suggests that the offense is not concealed to such an extent by the irrelevance of form that the latter has to be solved (as Bultmann claims) before the offense can be encountered. While the offense is implicit in the gospel message (kerygma), it is also implicit in the history of Israel, in the history of the church, in the exemplary lives of the servants of God, and in the doctrine and ethics consonant with their witness, all of which, because of their intelligibility, are less affected by the problem of irrelevance.

It cannot be denied that the problem of irrelevance is a serious problem. But it is not the whole problem and, if anything, is the lesser of two problems, the other of which is the offense of the Bible expressed in the manner in which its truth strikes the modern man, as indeed man in all times and places, as essentially alien. The two problems are, of course, always mixed up together. There is what we prefer to call the mystery content of the Bible (Bultmann's mythological content) and the intelligible content, between which there is no sharp dividing line, only a line that shifts in either direction, according to the degree of insight, but never so much that either content is swallowed up by the other. The offense belongs to both, although manifested more directly in the intelligible — which must not be confused with the rationalistic. The latter would eliminate the offense instead of communicating it.

In other words, this means the rejection in principle of Bultmann's proposal to " demythologize " the mystery content of the Bible, as an adequate solution of the problem of irrelevance. Our sympathy is with Bonhoeffer that such a proposal really resorts to the typical liberal reduction process (form separable from essence), and that the gospel message is not a mythological garbing of universal truth but that the so called mythological is the thing itself.[9] This is why we prefer to call it " mystery content "— to suggest that there is a content that is essentially incomprehensible and which is always necessarily so, and which therefore cannot be made intelligible. The boundary line between it and the intelligible content of the Bible can be pushed back to a considerable degree, but the center is never reached.

The strongest suggestion of the offense as the principal explanation of the closed Bible is the fact of the risk that is nearly always involved in a thorough interpretation. The frequency with which this occurs apart from any attempt at what Bultmann proposes is undoubtedly significant, and only understood on the basis of the potentially dangerous character of the great doctrines of the faith which constitute an important part of the intelligible content of the Bible. Even the parables, which in conventional exposition appear prosaic, were the subject matter of a message that contributed to Christ's death. What is involved is familiar to any serious ministry in its critical use of sources, its profound exploration of doctrine, its vital exposition of Scripture, and its courageous treatment of contemporary problems. It is a risk not primarily of popularity, of reputation, and of economic livelihood, but of a too deep involvement in the message and teaching of the Bible, particularly where these run counter to the accepted way of life. The avoidance of such a risk often seems, of course, from the point of view of a minister and from that of his people eminently rational and indicative of common sense. But what it signifies is best expressed in a penetrating remark of a contemporary theologian on the way in which ordinary, decent, reasonable people know that the way of the cross is a stumbling block and foolishness. " They insist," he says, " piously and quietly, but firmly and persistently, that they be spared the offense of the gospel and be presented instead with religion, orthodox or modern, which will not violate their most obvious and rational interests. . . . The gospel does look, to the mind of the flesh, a most unreasonable proposal and the people are determined not to make fools of themselves." [10]

3. Teaching as a Mediation of the Offense

In what respect can religion become an escape from the Biblical offense? This has to be answered before the claim is pressed that the teaching ministry is especially qualified to mediate the offense. The crux of the matter, to put it plainly, pertains to the ability of religion, particularly of the vacuous sort, to substitute itself for the Bible and in effect to promise all that the Bible can give. This possibility can only emerge from a self-sufficiency not unlike that of those ancient Corinthians whom the apostle Paul represented as saying: " Already we are filled! Already we are rich! Already we are kings! " (I Cor. 4:8). The open door which encourages it is therefore always some form of perfectionism in which faith is presumed to confer an adequacy which requires no supplementation. The " believer " is regarded as having no more serious problems, doubts, or sins, no more areas of ignorance or of immaturity that require the care of a pastor or teacher. In its most general form this is but the self-autonomous privacy of the claim that religion is only a matter between oneself and God, and even if there are problems, doubts, or sins, these are manageable — which, for practical purposes, is perfectionism. The characteristic conviction which therefore betrays the essential error is that the perfection is inherent in the " believer " rather than in the faithfulness of God. What this means is that the perfection is inherent in religion (experience) and not in grace. This explains the resistance to teaching and to a building up in the faith. Were it of grace, the resistance would vanish out of a recognition of a dependence upon God, and through him upon the fellowship of his people.

It is by its essential dishonesty that perfectionism (religion) provides an escape from the offense — a dishonesty not unlike that which the apostle Paul recognized in his former religion where he confessed that it was all a confidence in the flesh: " Circumcised the eighth day . . . a Hebrew of the Hebrews; as touching the law, a Pharisee; . . . touching the righteousness which is in the law, blameless. But what things were gain to me, those I counted loss for Christ " (Phil. 3:5-7). That is, when the essential dishonesty of his religion had been exposed, and like all religion brought to an end by the judgment of Christ, it created for him that relationship of grace which could perhaps be described as " religionless." Religion as perfectionism — and what variety of religion is free from it? — will always, however, resist such judgment, and, if necessary, exhibit a strange hardness of spirit if its citadel of self-righteousness is threatened.

At the level of ordinary religious practice this dishonesty may be detected in the inability to recognize what may be called the shadow side of faith. Accordingly, few of its followers will dare to be open and truthful with one another for fear of being accused of doubt or disloyalty, or of failing to conform to what is commonly accepted. If the possibility of being suspected of heresy be outmoded, the failure to be pragmatic may be feared as much, so that no one dares to deviate too obviously from such a norm. One cannot dare to be an Elijah who casts himself down at the foot of the juniper tree; one can only dare to be a Daniel. One cannot suffer the loneliness of Jeremiah, nor enter into the tragic dimensions of height and depth with which he understood his life and times; one can only rejoice in being a successful Joseph who rose to the top in Egypt. One cannot dare to be as honest as Job except in strictest privacy, and then only for a moment, for fear of feeling a sense of failure in one's religious life. One cannot cry out with one's Lord, "My God, my God, why hast thou forsaken me?" without being completely misunderstood and perhaps suspected of atheism.

It is now appropriate to inquire into the claim that the teaching ministry is especially qualified to mediate the offense — a claim which has been more frequently associated with preaching than with teaching. And by the teaching ministry we will mean not solely a separate, distinctive ministry, but one which interpenetrates all other ministries, inasmuch as their responsibility for truth never ceases. To put it as briefly and specifically as possible, the claim is that the teaching ministry is more likely to mediate the offense because of its capacity to stimulate thinking. This, of course, has to be qualified because there are various conceptions of thinking which could be confused with the one we have in mind, and thus invalidate our approach. Moreover, the possibility of thinking as a definite objective is somewhat unusual because few sermons and lessons aim to stimulate hard thinking. They do almost everything else — encourage reciting, memorizing, listening, feeling, or being inspired, comforted, reformed, or converted, but not thinking — at least not in that thoroughly searching and decisive manner which exercises the full vigor of the mind and, equally important, the integrity of the heart. Indeed, the fact that the Bible is especially able to fulfill such a purpose may come as a shock to those who have always associated it with obscurantism. So seldom has it been used for such a purpose that the possibility of its possessing a profound degree of intellectual relevance is almost nowhere recognized.

The first qualification of our conception is that churchmen should not be expected to think like academicians — which would be somewhat unnatural for them and frequently too specialized. They should only be expected to think within the context of their life and occupation as the Bible has relevance for them. This means that the theological terminology which is frequently of primary importance to the minister can only be used sparingly, in so far as it is germane to the Bible and susceptible of clarification. This should in no way be regarded as detracting from its highly important and definitive function in relation to his task, but only that it has to be carefully translated into the language and thought of his people as part of this task. In view of this qualification, our conception is not unlike that implied in the conversations of Jesus, which although deeply theological were couched in the language of concreteness and conducive to response. They caught up the participants in a form of thinking that involved not only the mind but the heart and the whole man in a confrontation of the Word from beyond (transcendental).

It will be obvious that our conception of thinking is different from that of the Socratic tradition which is always the objective of serious academicians. It is not an end in itself which can be encouraged on the assumption that man possesses within himself the truth in potential form, and therefore in principle the answer to all his problems. In Socratic thinking there is no offense — nothing that challenges the implicit norm presumed as constitutive of the nature of man (immanental). Therefore, it cannot be the task of the ministry of teaching to encourage participants only to think for the sake of thinking, as if by the exercise of thought ultimate answers could be excogitated. At the same time it cannot be emphasized enough that such a ministry does not have the Biblical offense at its disposal even though our phraseology may have suggested this fatal presumption. It has only one task — to open the meaning of the Biblical text with such diligence that it reads nothing extraneous into the text and, equally important, that it reads out of the text all that is in it, and in doing both to relate it to the real life of the people, which should be known as thoroughly as the text. Even this will not necessarily mean the communication of the offense any more than the stimulation of thinking, but with other things equal there is a greater likelihood that it will, because the teacher is honoring his task as a servant of the Word of God. In this capacity he will ask questions, point in specific directions, call things by their right names, and thus become an enemy of vacuity and vagueness, for no other reason than his obedience to the same Word who as incarnate also asked questions, pointed in specific directions, and called things by their right names.

4. *The Teacher and the Holy*

In such a role the teacher is less likely to be regarded as a holy man, because his interest in particularity and integrity is a threat, not only to vacuous religion as we have described it, but to that form of holiness which has divested itself of any concern for truth. In fact, this twofold interest of the teacher in particularity and integrity stands in a relation of tension to the traditional understanding of the holy which has to do with what is separated from or other than the profane. In this respect particularity (historical) and integrity (ethical) are somewhat the opposite of what is technically known as otherness. Even when the quality of otherness attaches to persons who can be named, there is a tension between it and the particularity that distinguishes them. This was why it was so difficult for the people of ancient Palestine to believe that Jesus of Nazareth could be the Christ. It also explains why students of theology often find it difficult to realize that the task of particularity which confronts them in reading, writing, thinking, and discussing specific problems may involve the holy quite as much as the worship in the chapel. In a similar manner, the quality of otherness that attaches to persons exists in tension with the integrity that distinguishes them. This was why it was so difficult for the people of ancient Palestine to believe that the Christ could have been at the same time the friend of publicans and sinners. As for the holy man who comes to be regarded as a teacher, the same resistance to his twofold interest will operate in the situation until at length as history proceeds his teaching role will tend to fall into the background in favor of roles that are more acceptably noumenal in character.

The effective reason for this reaction against the teacher, especially if he has come to be regarded as holy, is that his role always involves in one way or another an element of judgment. In a real sense a teacher is always a judge, no matter what his approach may be. He is one who makes demands, even though he clothes them in the delicate array of suggestion. Whatever else he may be, he is one who obligates. Above all, he asks questions. For those who wish to indulge in the religious life and worship without being confronted with any form of judgment, it is advisable to exclude the teacher from the sanctuary. To do this effectively and to eliminate the thin edge of the wedge by which the teacher might gain subtle access into the sanctuary, it is even more advisable to eliminate the true from the holy. This will provide additional assurance that any teacher whose integrity demands that he ask questions of ulti mate concern and which penetrate the worshipful atmosphere like a prophetic bolt of lightning will be excluded. In other words, the teacher who, in the context of the holy must of necessity become a prophet precisely because he particularizes God's ultimate concern for man, will be cast out of the temple. A form of worship will be preserved which can indulge itself in aesthetic and liturgical extravagance, cultivating a sense of wonder and of the desire to be lifted above the commoner things, but without being confronted by the realities of contemporary life, or by the specific sins of its participants and their need of repentance and forgiveness. A holiness that is not particularized by the prompting of prophetic integrity is powerless to confront man with his sin and the offer of forgiveness.

If we examine the role of Jesus as teacher, not only in Matthew and Luke, but in the whole Gospel tradition, it will be evident that it was in this particular role, so far as his contemporaries were concerned, that he was the most immediate challenge to Judaism. While his disciples divined that he was more than a teacher, and in the apostolic period saw him more especially as Lord and Savior, his contemporaries regarded him as a teacher who was troubling Israel. As for his outward appearance, approach, and habits, he resembled a Jewish rabbi who had his pupils and was bound to them and they to him by all those filial relationships characteristic of such a role. In this capacity he was exerting an influence which more and more aroused the suspicions of the Jewish religious authorities. It was what he was teaching and the authority associated with it that represented the focal point of the disturbance he was creating among them — not his claims to be more than a teacher, which, if anything, were concealed and left to his disciples and the people who heard him to gather indirectly for themselves. In other words, his teaching was the fleshly spearhead of the gospel. This does not mean, of course, that the content of his teaching was separated off from his Messianic significance and taught as general abstract truth per se, as liberalism has claimed. It means, rather, that his teaching and his role as teacher were the necessary and characteristic form in which his Messianic significance penetrated the stronghold of religion.

The various controversies in which he was involved with the Jewish religious leaders show this conclusively. These arose over basic issues — Sabbath observance, ceremonial purification, publicans and sinners, the interpretation of the Torah — in each of which the teaching of Jesus conflicted with the position of the religious leaders. In a number of respects the parables are a commentary upon these controversies and indicate the type of teaching which offended Jewish sensibilities. What this ultimately meant was that the issues thus raised so aroused the opposition of the Jews that they put Jesus to death. The truth, as represented by his teaching, and the authority associated with it, penetrated to such an extent and exposed so much that their reaction was one of anger. They determined they would destroy him. They eventually crucified him.

The role of Jesus as a teacher has not been sufficiently recognized as a role that, perhaps more than any other, contributed to his death. As a teacher he stood in the succession of the prophets whom Jerusalem had stoned and put to death because they spoke the truth so specifically and relevantly that guilty men knew what they were talking about. Even his enemies knew of his power as a teacher and the uncompromising way in which he delivered himself on important matters. This is evident in the satirical praise of the Pharisees: " Teacher, we know that you are true, and teach the way of God truthfully, and care for no man; for you do not regard the position of men " (Matt. 22:16). It is also evident in the congenial and well-meant compliment of Nicodemus: " Rabbi, we know that you are a teacher come from God " (John 3:2), as it is with the anxious probing of the high priest who questioned him about his disciples and his teaching (John 18:19).

This observation is important because it establishes a connection between the teaching ministry of Jesus and the cross. It reminds us of the well-known truth that all great teachers are dangerous. They always ask the kind of questions that compel accepted belief to re-examine itself. They not only scrutinize established tradition, they establish new tradition. They assume the same responsibility for the communication of truth as they do for its discovery.

In making these observations we distinguish such teachers from others who claim the name. They are not as the *scribes,* who are the copyists, the lovers of precedent, whose aim is to transmit the truth with as little change as possible, and whose pride is to preserve every jot and tittle. They are not as the *apologists,* who are devoted to the defense of truth and who as masters of argument seek to commend it to those who would assail it. Nor are they *propagandists,* who are on the offensive because they see the truth as something of use for social control and who are always anxious for the reader to draw the desired conclusion from officially approved material. Nor are they *sophists,* more interested in the question than in the answer, and only in the answer in so far as it can be presumably extracted from the learner. Nor are they *research scholars,* so interested in the discovery of truth that they assume no responsibility for its communication, or for its significance in the total perspective of man.

In various respects they share with these a common heritage and the insight that comes of sound learning and the integrity of mind and heart. But in one important respect they differ — chiefly because it involves their understanding of truth. They know, as all great teachers know, that truth is costly, and that the price to be paid is the price of suffering — not merely the suffering that follows on behalf of the truth, but the suffering that comes of truth itself, when the burden is not from others, for fear of what they will do, but from the responsibility that truth imposes. In fact, the more significant the truth, the greater the suffering, because in every case our conception of what a teacher is and of the task he performs is determined by our conception of the truth. From this observation it is no great leap of logic to say that the incarnation by its nature is such as would lead to the cross. As the Word of God made flesh, it is the corporate form of the One who could say not only " I know the truth," but, "I am the truth." A teacher who could say this could expect the severest kind of suffering, and this at the same time would distinguish him from others who also claimed to be teachers.

In spite of such reflections as these, which prompt us to ask what a teacher is and to realize that the answer depends upon the particular conception of truth we hold, and which the discussion suggests should be Biblically determined, it is surprising how frequently in theological literature, and perhaps even more of late, a teacher is regarded almost exclusively as a purveyor of abstract content. The impression thus created is that of a teacher who always stands to some extent outside the faith, adopting, as it were, an objective approach, and who, as a result, is partial to the concept that knowledge is always somewhat impersonal. It would be absurd, of course, to deny that a teacher is of necessity involved in such a role, which is so intimately associated with thorough research and scholarship. A teacher who is not a master of abstract content is no teacher at all. But the point is that we cannot stop here in our conception of a teacher. We must widen it to include the kind of truth that is identical with wisdom, and which in its Biblical sense is close to what we have indicated by integrity, particularly if we think of integrity as the analogue of the faithfulness of God. A teacher in the Biblical sense of the term, however great his mastery of abstract content, is no teacher at all except he be prompted always by a prophetic consciousness of integrity.[11]

The Domestication of the Bible

1. *The Cult of Simplicity*

Since it is evident that the subordination of the teaching ministry involves the subordination of the Bible and this to such an extent that it jeopardizes the future of the Bible in the life and work of the church, we now examine the process by which this tragic possibility usually develops. In general we characterize it as the domestication of the Bible, but more specifically as a form of irresponsible simplification which in its corporate expression is perhaps akin to what might be called a cult of simplicity. Its most obvious manifestation is that of a facile spirit which is capable of emptying the Bible and the best theology of content so that no mystery remains, no necessity of hard thinking, no rending of the heart, no suffering in order to understand, and no dying in order to live.

It is only wisdom, therefore, in the life and thought of the church, and no less in that of the individual, to be always cautious of the facile. At this point, there seems to be the greatest warrant for the Scriptural injunction to try the spirits whether they are of God. For it is evident that we cannot assume that all simplification is good or that the slightest benefit is any adequate justification irrespective of possible harmful effects. For there is no gainsaying the fact that the concept of simplification is extremely ambiguous. We can make of it almost anything we will — equate it with the best pedagogical wisdom of a teacher who interprets the profoundest spirituality in the language of a child, or with the glib tongue of an ecclesiastical buffoon whose treatment of the sacred text reduces it to nonsense. In the best sense, truly to simplify is truly to teach. It means that the task of simplification is nothing other than the task of interpretation accepted with a due sense of responsibility for both the adequacy of the truth and the humanity of the hearer. Its secret will be found less in the clarity attained than in the responsibility that determines it. Without such responsibility it deteriorates into the facile. If we may express it paradoxically, to make things truly simple is extremely difficult. It requires a great knowledge of subject matter and a depth of insight which few possess. Only the great masters really know how to simplify.

The commonest error, however, and one that opens the door to incalculable mischief, is the assumption that it is simple to simplify, a task for which few qualifications are required. In this case the would-be teacher is irresponsible. He is not concerned that the result of his simplification adequately represent the complexity he claims to have simplified. The question of the representative function of the simple does not trouble his conscience. Correspondence between the simple and what it is intended to simplify is not a problem for him. The ease with which he accepts an approximation of the two is a measure of his irresponsibility.

The appeal for simplicity is, of course, a powerful one, not only because of its popularity but because of its Biblical attestation. For there is an obvious simplicity in the Bible which commends itself to the humblest reader — the poetic simplicity of the psalms, the homely simplicity of the proverbs, the vivid metaphorical simplicity of the sayings of Jesus and his parables. There is the emphatic appeal of the apostle Paul that babes in

Christ should be fed the milk of the word and not at first the solid meat. There is his warning lest the gospel be proclaimed in the lofty language of worldly wisdom. Not to recognize this Biblical emphasis on the need for simplicity is to obstruct the Word of God and to fail in love toward one's hearers. It is no different from recourse to an unknown tongue which, because it fails to edify the people, deserves the pointed remark of Paul to the ancient Corinthians that in the church he would rather speak five words with his understanding in order that he might teach others, than ten thousand words in an unknown tongue (I Cor. 14:19).

But what Paul is talking about is a responsible simplicity which is only the steppingstone to a fuller and richer knowledge of the truth, not a simplicity that closes the door against such knowledge, not a simplicity that suggests that the babes in Christ have resolved always to remain as babes and never to feed on anything other than milk. For the peculiar thing about the irresponsible simplification of the Bible is the extent to which it is permeated by a refusal to mature. Everything must be kept easy and reassuring without being disturbed by the claims of Biblical truth and the basic problems of human existence. A scholarly minister will be dubbed as "bookish" just as a gifted student will be dubbed a "brain." His children's story will be better appreciated than his sermon. Creeds and confessions will be disparaged in favor of what is called a simple allegiance to the Bible, but which has little concern with the intelligible content of the Bible. A serious interest in Biblical theology will be taken as evidence of an "ivory tower" mentality, which is likely to stifle the spontaneity of simple faith and which, because it is alleged to be out of touch with life, is by no means considered in the frontal line of action occupied by those so busily engaged in the work of Christ that they never have time to read.

Such an attitude is unfortunately justified in part by the adverse reputation intellectualism has had in certain periods of the history of the church and from which the teaching ministry has never been completely free because of the unavoidable intellectual nature of its task. The familiar epithets applied to intellectualism each tell their story. Intellectualism tends to be dry, cold, barren, abstract, impersonal, fragmented, uncommitted, and divorced from life. Its perennial temptation of equating the meaning of faith with assent to doctrine has been justly questioned by those who know that faith involves a personal relationship with a living Lord; its contemplative, spectator attitude, by those who know that faith involves an urgency which comes of total commitment. Its presumption of being able to think its way through to God has been justly questioned by those who know that God is not an object of thought but the subject of grace; its fragmentation of truth and life, by those who know that the wholeness of each is the blessing of God.

Yet with all that can be justly said against intellectualism, an irresponsible simplification is not the answer. There is no hope in undercutting the intelligible content of the Bible in the interest of a subjectivity which assumes that what a man thinks in the house of God is of less importance than what he feels. A cult of simplicity can be just as dangerous as a cult of intellectuality. For if the temptation of the latter is its proneness toward the legalism implicit in all logical thought, the temptation of the former is its proneness toward the opposite of legalism — the antinomianism implicit in the charismatic divorced from truth. In other words, the cult of simplicity tends to lawlessness. It wants love without justice, repentance without restitution, freedom without discipline, gospel without law. Its irresponsible attitude to truth undermines order and rigor of thought in the life and work of the church. It is as if the ancient antinomians had said to the apostle Paul: " Since by thinking we attain not unto salvation, we will do no thinking. Let us be ignorant that grace may abound." [12]

2. *The Domestication of the Bible*

a. Conversionism

If now we turn to the first of several forms of simplification that subordinate the teaching ministry, it will probably occasion surprise that we begin with the familiar conception of a saving knowledge of the Bible. We do this not with any desire to minimize its importance, but to deepen and enrich its meaning in the hope that the weakness from which it often suffers, the divorce of grace from truth, of Spirit from Word, may be as far as possible overcome. The implicit problem which calls for discussion is the facile line that is frequently drawn between a saving knowledge of the Bible and a substantial knowledge. According to the popular description, a saving knowledge is a warm, personal commitment to Christ which need not involve more than a few texts or themes; a substantial knowledge is a cold, impersonal grasp of an intellectual content, always somewhat complex in nature but without commitment. The argument runs as follows: Since it is possible for a relatively illiterate man to acquire a saving knowledge of the Bible with only a limited knowledge of its substance, a substantial knowledge is only of secondary importance. Therefore a saving knowledge is by definition a relatively simple knowledge within the reach of everyone, which requires little or no intellectual apprehension of Biblical content. Its intellectual component is reduced to a minimum. At the same time a substantial knowledge is not regarded as integral to faith. Biblical theology as such has little or no saving efficacy.

The extent, however, to which this familiar argument makes man the measure of simplicity is greater than we realize, as will be seen in the arbitrary manner in which it distinguishes the two forms of knowledge on the basis of a preconceived idea of simplicity. The line between them is drawn in such a way that a saving knowledge is always simple according to the standards of popular religion, which are more of our own making and more accommodated to self-interest than we are prepared to admit. It is our idea of the simple that too often enters into our understanding of the simplicity of a saving knowledge. And because it is our idea, it can often be a form of escape from God, who in his purpose to save would confront us with a more complex knowledge of the Bible than we care to face, not so much because of intellectual difficulty, although this will be involved, but because the truth hurts and the Word, like a two-edged sword, penetrates to the dividing asunder of our soul and spirit, our joints and marrow (Heb. 4:12).

Humanly speaking, it depends upon the circumstances whether a saving knowledge in the form of a simple grasp of a text or theme is efficacious, or whether a substantial knowledge is efficacious. We cannot be arbitrary about it. The former may be sufficient for an unlearned man who under stress and strain finds in a single text the flash of insight which, as the revelation of God, is the difference between life and death. But the latter may be necessary for the same man under different circumstances, or for a learned man whose knowledge of history, philosophy, science, religion, and life can only be challenged by a penetration of the Biblical substance in depth. For him a substantial knowledge of the Bible may be the only saving knowledge. Indeed he may be continually in revolt against the superficiality of the sectarian idea of what constitutes a saving knowledge. Therefore we must not assume in an arbitrary way that theology and scholarship, including even a knowledge of Greek and Hebrew, are not necessary for a saving knowledge.

The habit of justifying the opposite point of view by appealing to the fact that early Christianity attracted the poor, humble, and unlearned in contrast to the privileged and the learned, overlooks the fact that the early Christians, as well as the writers of the Scripture itself, frequently exhibited unusual intellectual power. What kind of congregation was it in Rome, for example, which could appreciate the intellectual intricacy of Paul's argument in the epistle to the Romans? And what kind of man was Paul to write it? Or what kind of man was the writer of The Book of Job, with its literary excellence and its depth of insight into the spiritual aspects of the problem of suffering? Or what of Jeremiah — the complexities of his life and times and the richness and depth of his message? Or what of the parables with their strangely inexhaustible profundity despite an external simplicity? The writers of the Bible were not superficial simpletons who scratched the surface of life any more than they were pedantic experts who manipulated insignificant minutiae. They were thinkers who thought profoundly — not as those who began with themselves, but with God, not with abstract ideas, but with the concreteness of history and of everyday life.

What leaves the door open for the tempting assumption that a saving knowledge of the Bible is of necessity a superficial knowledge, is the claim that the Bible can be sufficiently understood by the plain reader without the aid of scholarship and therefore without the aid of a teacher in the more serious sense of the term. The plain reader with his Bible is regarded as capable of grasping all that is necessary for eternal salvation. The implications of such a conception are at once obvious in relation to the ministry and to the church. The autonomy of the plain reader ultimately means that in principle he recognizes no need of the ministry or of the church. He is alone with God as he is with his Bible — a situation that may be resolved in either of two directions — in the liberalistic emphasis on the right of private judgment or the sectarian emphasis on the same judgment informed of the Holy Spirit, particularly for the interpretation of difficult passages. In such a mood the seriously minded plain reader of the Bible tends to substitute prayer and meditation for the necessary intellectual effort of which he is capable, and which the Bible, by the nature of its content, properly demands. This does not mean that prayer and meditation are unimportant, but only that in such circumstances they are misplaced, because they relieve the reader of effort and often of the hard thinking that constitutes obedience to God's word. He is disposed to believe that he does not need to consult commentaries, concordances, dictionaries, and other aids. When such a disposition is expressed in practice it means that the kind of scholarship and Biblical theology that is always the presupposition of an effective teaching ministry is undercut. As a result, the typical preacher is the lay preacher, from whom it is not a great step to the lay teacher of the Sunday school movement.

b. Biblicism

Another form of simplification involved in the subordination of the teaching ministry is one that has to do with the transformation of the Bible into a thing of itself, and therefore out of relation to every significant context. It is really only the old error on a grand scale of lifting an item out of the context of relationship that gives it meaning, which in the case of the Bible means all aspects of its historical background: religious, political, economic, including ideological and cosmological perspectives and daily life of the people. The Biblical text is endowed with the same autonomy possessed by the plain reader and is presumed to depend no more upon its background than he upon the church.

The effect this has upon the truth of the Bible is of particular interest because it indicates the purpose of the simplification at the practical level, which is that of rendering the truth as safe as possible. The same truth which heretofore was regarded as saving truth is, according to this further phase of simplification, now regarded as safe truth. In so far as it involves the individual in a risk, it is limited to the spiritual as distinct from the material, to the subjective as distinct from the objective. This follows from the fact that the truth, as a thing of itself, is separated off from real life.

How this happens at the practical level will be suggested by the familiar advice to preach the gospel and abstain from politics — advice that is pertinent enough for those who would substitute politics for gospel, but the worst counsel for those whose gospel would make no difference to politics. It is when we consider the range and variety of those things from which preachers have been advised to abstain that we feel the full impact of what the advice involves — politics, economics, social welfare, racial differences, to mention only a few of the larger areas of concern. Add to these the smaller areas of private life where the most acute personal problems arise, add the areas of cultural interest and endeavor which are so frequently unrelated to the message of the Bible, and the variety is so great that the sum total is almost equivalent to real life itself, where issues of importance are being decided every hour of the day.

If, under these circumstances, the preacher remains loyal to the Bible, a strong temptation arises of entering into its world accompanied by his people, so that they may all live together in this world on Sunday morning in a comfortable, Utopian fashion. But it will not be the Biblical world as the prophets and apostles and Christ himself knew it, where their messages were not abstracted from the vital issues of contemporary society nor protected from the menacing challenge of dark pow-

ers, religions, and philosophies. It will be a reconstructed Biblical world in which the preacher and his people may move
around as they please, idealize here and there, pick and choose
their favorite items, and thus avoid the basic questions for
which the ancient servants of God forfeited their lives. Super-
ficially, at least, it will have the appearance of a thorough commitment to the Bible, especially as familiar texts are quoted,
favorite stories recited, and these servants of God eulogized.
Everything will be praised but kept within the accepted limits
of safety. The role of the preacher and his people will be essentially that of spectators, who are interested in a great drama of
the past and who in various ways identify themselves with its
leading characters and relive with them what is presumed to
have been their crucial experiences. But it will seldom lead to
decisive action, because the relevance to the important issues of
daily life has been so largely nullified in the interests of safety.

In this respect the critical, scientific approach with its incip-
ient positivism is no improvement, because, as another form
of Biblicism, it substitutes the autonomy of facts for the autonomy of texts. To a large extent the Biblical content is fragmented into an assortment of details, with a variety of footnotes
but which leave unanswered the problem of piecing them together and indicating their relevance to life. The situation thus
created serves the interests of safety as much as ever, because
with the fragmentation of the Biblical content no one quite
knows what the Bible is saying. All assertions of its truth tend
to become provisional. The preacher does not have to abstain
from politics and economics or from other areas of concern because he is less certain of what he would say if he did make
the venture. At the same time he can retire into the Biblical
world, not as an excursionist into the past, but as one engaged
in research. He can move freely around in such a world, choos-
ing his favorite items and searching for facts but without in-

volvement in vital issues. The simplification thus achieved is the same as for any creative production subjected to a scientific analysis. It is a question of the wisdom we lose in knowledge and the knowledge we lose in information.[13]

c. Moralism

The commonest form of simplification is the one implicit in the moralism that has characterized the literature of the Sunday school and the substance of popular preaching. To understand it we must view the moralism out of which it arises not so much in the thorough, legitimate sense of an ethic of duty as a moralism that fails to take itself seriously because it is meant more for children than for adults; and when for adults, more for the uncouth and the socially unacceptable. The facile spirit may be seen in the ease with which it defines the good, in the confidence with which it presumes to achieve it, and in the naïveté with which it reduces the personal and the historical to the level of propositional statement without realizing that anything has been lost in the process. Such a spirit is nowhere more clearly exposed for what it is than on those critical and ofttimes tragic occasions when a man becomes deeply aware of the problem he is to himself for which no moralism, and certainly not of the popular variety, can provide the answer. World War II supplied us with many examples of sincere young men and women whose disillusionment with what they supposed was the substance of the Christian faith began at this point.

In this form of simplification the search is always for rules, principles, ideals, something that can be extracted like the kernel from the husk, an objective that can be achieved, set out as a practical program, measured, talked about, and reported upon. Such a tendency is revealed in the use of the moralistic vocabulary, in which each term — pride, humility, greed, and generosity, as the case may be — is presumed to possess a single, easily recognized, commonly accepted meaning, with no recognition of the fact that in actual circumstances each may have a dozen different meanings. The same irresponsible simplification applied to the Ten Commandments regards each commandment as embodying one self-evident, unambiguous principle, the exceptions to which are either presumed not to exist or conveniently obscured. "Thou shalt not kill" is often assumed to be as simple in meaning as two and two in primary mathematics, and susceptible of no difficulty when it comes to the question of whether war and capital punishment are not patent violations of it. No less important a passage than the Sermon on the Mount suffers the same extreme simplification as the commandments. There is the same tendency to reduce it to a few self-evident principles such as turning the other cheek or lending to him that asks — both of which are not infrequently represented as the secret of success, and this incredible result in a highly competitive social and economic order. In other interpretations obviously more ambitious in character, the Sermon is advertised as a remarkable platform of world-wide peace, with one important proviso — if the nations only obey it. The Golden Rule, which is the favorite of them all and for many the sum and substance of everything, is happily reduced to a convenient moral relativity according to which the likes of a man define for him his duty to others. By the same token each is presumed to know what is good for himself. All of this assures the popularity of the rule. For who would fail to applaud an ethical principle which, were a man to desire wine, women, and song as the highest good, would oblige him to seek it for others, in the knowledge that they would seek it for him?

The simplified Christology which corresponds to such moralism admits of a variety of interpretations, two of which, the patron and the ideal, are more pertinent than the others — the former embodying the role of a gentle guarantor of conventional goodness, the latter a personification of religious success. As a patron of what one assumes to be good for oneself and for others, which will be largely identified with accepted standards, Christ becomes at the same time the patron of the established order, the guarantor of its way of life. As an ideal, his principal function is that of inspiring others to approximate the religious success he is presumed to have had. Since he stands for the same facile goodness, which by virtue of the Golden Rule each man defines for himself, any exhortation to be Christlike tends to be identified with the actualization of self-interest. When the identification is finally complete, so that the striving for Christlikeness is indistinguishable from self-realization, the door is opened to psychologism at the expense of the Biblical content. Under these circumstances, the cultivation of personality and of the subjective life becomes the primary object and indeed the norm of the Biblical content. The psychology of religion becomes the master key of theology. At this point the process of simplification is nothing other than the quest of an underlying psychological explanation of every doctrine and passage of Scripture. The preacher assumes that his main task is that of comforting, encouraging, and reassuring his people, with little concern for the objectivity of Biblical truth. Instead of moralizing in the older, conventional sense, he psychologizes and neglects the ever-important task of accurate exegesis.

When we see how moralism tends to work itself out into psychologism we will appreciate why impressionism has become so normative in the life and work of the church. For impressionism involves the subordination of the intelligible, in the identification of the good with feeling. The decisive question which it prompts of any policy or course of action is,

Does it make a favorable impression? The appropriateness of worship and the effectiveness of preaching will be determined solely by this standard. New members will be admitted less because of the substance and integrity of their faith than by their ability to convince the congregation of being desirables. New ministers will be called less because of their record of achievement and the maturity and relevance of their message than by the winsomeness of their personality. At almost every turn impressionism will take the place of confessionalism. The conviction will steadily grow: it is better to impress than to confess.

3. Simplification and Religious Security

Our discussion to this point indicates that in three of the commonest forms of simplification religious security is of greater importance than Biblical knowledge. The preference in each case is for only enough Biblical knowledge to give the desired security. The learner turns to the Bible only enough to find a limited amount of obviously simple knowledge which stirs his emotions and gives him assurance, but beyond this he has little interest in the Bible. We have seen, for example, that a saving knowledge is regarded in principle as a simple knowledge, and that in so far as it is looked upon as complete it discourages the acquisition of a substantial knowledge. The religious security that many obtain through the conversion experience satisfies them to such an extent that their interest in the Bible does not advance much beyond those favorite texts and passages associated with their conversion. The same tendency appears in Biblicism, but in a different form. The learner looks to the Bible as a symbol of security, whose truth is safe and which, because it is not permitted to impinge upon real life and to challenge it, tends to be regarded as sanctioning the *status quo* and upholding those institutions which contribute to stability — the home, the school, the courts of law, and the state. As the worshiper retires into the reconstructed, Utopian Biblical world as a religious exercise, he experiences a feeling of security and finds himself stabilized. But here, as before, it is more for the satisfaction of his need than for the increase of his knowledge, more for the release from fear and anxiety than for the hearing of God's word. In moralism, the experience of security arises out of a feeling of achievement, out of the satisfaction of having achieved the good at a practical level in meritorious conduct, which is pleasing both to man and to God. This is the religious aspect of the security. But since the meaning of the good is often little more than a blind acceptance of the best standards of secular society, the moralistic emphasis on being good usually ends in social conformity. In so far as the individual has the courage to be himself it may end in self-realization. In any case the primary interest is in security and not in Biblical content. Only those portions of the Bible which lend themselves most readily to a moralistic treatment tend to be used — the rest of the Bible tends to be neglected.

It would be a mistake, however, to limit our thinking to religious security as if it were an isolated phenomenon and not intimately connected with other forms of security — political, economic, social, and psychological, the total complex of which is so characteristic of everyday life. For we have seen at various points how the question of religious security merges itself with this larger question of security, making it impossible to deal with the one without the other. What has to be understood, therefore, is that the simplification of Biblical truth in the interest of security is never a matter only of religious security but of all forms of security. It is the adaptation of Biblical truth for the purpose of justifying and enhancing all forms and seldom, if ever, for the purpose of challenging them. It is the assimilation of Biblical truth to the ideological situation which is often implied in speaking of securities and which as such is their quasi-religious or cultic expression. In one society this may mean the assimilation of Biblical truth to feudalism, in another to capitalism, in another to socialism, with all the variations which in each case arise from differing historical circumstances.

Contemporary North American Christianity is no exception to this. The commoner forms of simplification which are conspicuous in its pulpits and classrooms involve to a greater degree than realized the adaptation of Biblical truth to the ideological situation. Biblical truth is subordinated in the interest of a religious security which is at the same time surprisingly identified with the securities provided by the secular world. The extent to which, under these circumstances, a devotion to religion may be accompanied by a devotion to secularism even in the same person is often amazing. Proof of this general assimilation of religion to the secular order may be seen in the extent to which the benefits of faith are regarded as coinciding with the secular philosophy of success, in the case of conversionism, Biblicism, and moralism alike. In each case the believer is represented as a success in religion — not in the New Testament understanding of suffering and persecution, an offense to contemporary society, but in terms of what the prevailing ideology defines as success — prosperity, position, and peace of mind. Even at the level of national life the promise is made that if we repent, the nuclear bombs will not fall, the implication of which is that repentance is the means by which our secular success may be guaranteed and enhanced. But in this there is little inclination to recognize that the really terrifying issues of our day may be implicit in such success even in its baptized form, and that real repentance ought to challenge it at this point no less than at any other.

The full significance of the adaptation of Biblical truth to the ideological situation becomes apparent only when it is seen in the larger perspective of the religious life of the contemporary world and the trends that characterize it. It is only a special phase of that larger subordination of the church's intellectual task by the noumenal, mystical, psychological, and pragmatical, whose disparagement of theology is well known. In another sense it is a reflection of that subordination of all genuinely intellectual endeavor and of the dignity of the teaching profession, which until recently has been so characteristic of the popular ethos of the street and of the market place. But in another and a more serious sense it is evidence within the church of that dissolution of tradition which is taking place within the general cultural situation of the contemporary world, as a result of which the individual is losing his roots and merging himself with the amorphous masses of a collectivized society. Fearful of freedom, of ultimate decision, of accepting responsibility for himself, he prefers to lose himself in the crowd in an undifferentiated togetherness. On this basis, denominational differences tend to disappear, not so often because of a greater tolerance, or a greater ecumenicity, as because of a loss of the particular tradition that characterized the denomination. The same thing happens with the deeper differences separating the Catholic, Protestant, and Jew.[14] As these tend to disappear, Catholic, Protestant, and Jew become more and more alike in terms of a religiosity largely devoid of content, but which is the spiritualized expression of their common loyalty to the secular way of life, considerably colored by nationalism. We need but expand our perspective a little to see the same process tending to dissolve the distinctive features of each of the great world religions, making it possible at length to cross from one to the other with the same facility that many now cross from one denomination to the other — all in terms of a vacuous religiosity.[15] The extent to which this dissolution of tradition is occuring is difficult to determine, but of one thing we are certain. Like the old syncretism of earlier centuries now reinforced by the critical subtlety and technique of the modern world, it confronts us on a vaster scale than ever before. Although certain factors work against it, not the least of which is its own lack of vitality as a common-denominator religion and, in contrast to this, the surprising resurgence of confessionalism, these are not sufficient assurance that time is not on its side.

Turning now to the church as an institution, and the extent to which it is identified with the interests of secular security, it will be recognized that in such a capacity it not only subserves the individual but is served by him. The interrelationship between the security of the individual and that of the institution is one of mutual reinforcement. Above all, the church as an institution requires money, buildings, equipment, and personnel in order to maintain itself and provide the kind of security the individual expects from it. As such it requires loyalty to itself, comprising financial support and co-operation in its various projects. As the individual meets these conditions he finds a greater security for himself because he is more readily accepted within the life and work of the church.

But the extent to which the mutual reinforcement of security will have any substantial reference to the Bible is likely to be only nominal, as the various forms of irresponsible simplification show. For what they have in common — the one characteristic that indicates that in a large measure they are all forms of the same thing — is their failure to come to grips with the solid substance of the Bible. The implicit, somewhat unconscious assumption is that as long as the institution is successful in the maintenance of itself, including the reinforcement of the religious security of its members, no great concern over the Bible is necessary. As long as there is sufficient attention to the Bible to sanction institutional success, little more is needed. The Bible in this sense is therefore less a means of grace than a symbolical sanction of all that is done. Thus a situation is created in which religious experience and loyalty to the institution are consolidated in an alliance which reverences the Bible as an object of veneration, but which does not choose to enter into its rich and challenging substance.

The religious experience on the basis of which this happens is typical of what may be called " folk religion." By "folk religion " we mean that piety of the people which is more or less universal in its popularity, a kind of vacuous common denominator of all religions, always more religious than it is Christian and mystically grounded in the social, national, and racial consciousness. More concerned with feeling than with thought, it tends to be impatient of theology and of the intellectual formulation of faith and why the identity of God should matter. The nameless, nebulous, all-pervasive noumenal implicit in the spirit of the people and explicit in their way of life is a sufficient definition of his existence. One is therefore urged to turn to a higher power but never to be curious about it, to praise the God from whom all blessings flow but never to ask, what God? One is advised to pray to him and to commune with him but to leave aside all questions difficult to answer. Theology can only disturb. Biblical study can only be a speculative pursuit because no one has the final word. If one is disposed to interrogate in an honest desire to seek the truth, one is flatly reminded that God exists with the same certainty that the earth is spherical and the sun sets in the west. Something higher and greater than oneself exists — call it what you will. Therefore fall down and worship it. In the end, the main thing is the practical — the happiness, the prosperity, and the success which the pursuit of piety inspired by such a God will surely bring.[16]

If one looks at such a nebulous religion as a whole, it will not be difficult to recognize how much it has simplified everything in the interest of security. The process of simplification is in this case integral to the meaning of security. Simplification is only another name for the gradual dissolution of the kerygmatic and didactic tradition of the church, the disintegration of theology, the disappearance of what is distinctive of the Christian faith, in the interests of a nebulous natural religion which for this reason is better able to offer the kind of security that is the goal of the secular world. The distinctiveness of the Christian faith which is always preserved by a church that hears what the Bible has to say to it is thereby threatened. More specifically, it is the Bible itself that is threatened.

4 | Relational Hermeneutics

1. *The Influence of Positivism*

The subordination of the teaching ministry is ultimately a hermeneutical problem. For whatever may be said of good pedagogy and of a humane regard for the learner, there is no substitute for the solid Biblical content which is of relevance to life and which it is the task of the interpreter to ponder as he translates the truth of the Bible into the language of the common man. Every minister and student who looks for this solid content in the place where he has a right to expect it, in the Biblical commentaries, and turns away disappointed because they too often fail to provide it, will know where the problem of his teaching ministry begins. He will have discovered that it begins at the point where interpretation begins, because interpretation is of the essence of teaching and Biblical interpretation the fountainhead of the teaching ministry. This does not mean a right to expect the commentator to provide ready-made sermons or spelled-out applications of truth, because the task of interpretation is not the transmission of material relatively unchanged in the process, but a creative communication in which the dead is made alive, the old new, and the learner provided with a quality of insight which makes him wise. The teaching ministry accordingly is not only a service unto knowledge, important as this is, but more important still, a service unto wisdom. If it has failed in either respect, a considerable part of the responsibility must be borne by the positivistic commentators, who as scholars have often been less than teachers in the specialized sense of interpreting the Bible to those who will interpret it to others.

The commentator may object that this is not his task, because his responsibility is only that of discovering the truth and not its communication. He may claim that it is only that of laying bare the facts regardless of their pertinence or application to contemporary life, which in his opinion is for the theologian, preacher, or teacher. In support of his argument he can appeal to the tradition of free inquiry, which refuses to submit to prejudice in any form, be it that of unexamined belief or the subservience of truth to practical ends. He will have on his side the achievements of free inquiry which have contributed to the advancement of science and technical progress. But this is not all. He can appeal to the tradition of loyalty to the Biblical text which has characterized the work of distinguished commentators through the centuries. He can insist that he is in harmony with those who in all periods of the history of the church have begun and ended with what the Biblical text says of itself, and who have sought to guard it against the importation of extraneous meanings. He can insist that his only concern is to find in the text the meaning indigenous to it, and to engage in an exegesis which, according to the derivation of the term, extracts a deposit of truth somewhat after the fashion of a prospector who extracts gold from the ore, or of a chemist who extracts a drug from a capsule, always making certain that nothing from without contaminates it. Thus, in his loyalty to historicism with its emphasis on the scientific approach, he can appeal to Biblicism, because both have in principle the same conception of truth — truth as a quantum which is laid down in Scripture analogous to a mineral deposit in the crust of the earth.

It is not difficult to see that the problem of a subordinate teaching ministry is accentuated by such a conception of exegesis, because no matter whether the commentator is concerned with facts or texts, the truth he discovers is a thing of itself, the communication of which bears no inward relationship to the discovery. The discovery is one thing, the communication another. The communication is only incidental to the discovery. For even though the commentator discovers the truth, his task is in principle completed because he is not obliged, as far as his conception of truth is concerned, to communicate it. He may, and probably will, communicate it, but his compulsion to do so is external to the discovery and subsequent to it. He will not regard the communication as a further phase of discovery as necessary for a knowledge of the truth as the initial phase itself, and without which he has no right to claim that he has really discovered the truth. Everything instead, according to his conception, will end with the initial discovery so that the communication is only a matter of the transmission of units complete in themselves, as capsules of truth, be they facts or texts.

What this means for the teaching ministry will be even clearer if it is remembered that the subordination of communication is at the same time the subordination of interpretation, because the two are interrelated. The commentator in his preoccupation with discovery will not regard interpretation as his task. Indeed, if consistent, he will tend to regard it as a secondary task, perhaps as no task at all, because truth for him in the form of self-contained units is immediately recognizable. Since facts are facts, and texts are texts, the truth is directly revealed without the necessity of interpretation. On this basis neither the task of the theologian, nor that of the preacher, still less that of the teacher, has much relevance because communication has been reduced to a mechanical transmission, a recital of facts and texts, a saying of right words and phrases, which the hearer by virtue of the supposed immediacy of their truth will presumably recognize and accept. Thus on the basis of the positivism both of the Biblical scholar and of the Biblicist we have an explanation of the tendency on the part of the church to expect a hearing by merely repeating a sacred vocabulary, with a minimum of interpretation. When the hearer fails to hear and to understand, it is seldom recognized how much of the difficulty has arisen from the conception of truth as a thing of itself, which, because it is separated off from all considerations of context, including everyday life, is by definition already irrelevant.[17]

The problem may be illustrated from any average commentary in its preoccupation with isolated units of truth left in a fragmented form without being used as the material of a treatment which would develop the meaning of the passage. The disconnected notes on places, names, metric equivalents, peculiar words, idioms, and construction, which are presented to the reader as of paramount importance, are often peripheral to the main theme of the passage, which as its *raison d'être* seems not to have attracted the interest of the commentator. An occasional reference to a fine shade of meaning will arouse the reader's expectation of serious interpretation, but only until he sees it as an isolated insight, unrelated to the main thrust of meaning which has probably been ignored. At times there seems to be almost an aversion to serious interpretation, as though a knowledge of vocabulary had robbed the commentator of a knowledge of concepts.

On the familiar parable of the good Samaritan, for example, the usual notes on priests and Levites, roads and robbers, village inns and monetary units, will be provided. Peculiar words, qualified by the phrase " Here only in the New Testament," will always be recognized. A relatively minor point like the difference in conduct between priest and Levite will probably receive attention in preference to the important matter of their motivation with regard to their conception of holiness, of legal responsibility, and of neighborliness. The speculative question as to whether the Samaritan was original to the parable is likely to receive more attention than the extremely important question of how his radical love transcended the Jewish law and at the same time modern humanitarianism. If included at all, the treatment of the ethical significance of the parable will be perfunctory and couched in the language of conventional morality.

These observations bear a resemblance to those of Barth in the preface to the second edition of his commentary on Romans, which emphasizes the seriousness of the problem:

" My complaint," he says, " is that recent commentators confine themselves to an interpretation of the text which seems to me to be no commentary at all, but merely the first step towards a commentary. Recent commentaries contain no more than a reconstruction of the text, a rendering of Greek words and phrases by the precise equivalents, a number of additional notes in which archaeological and philological material is gathered together, and a more or less plausible arrangement of the subject matter in such a manner that it may be made historically and psychologically intelligible from the standpoint of pure pragmatism. . . .

" When, however, I examine their attempts at genuine understanding and interpretation, I am again and again surprised at how little they even claim for their work. . . .

" For me at any rate, the question of the true nature of interpretation is the supreme question — or is it that these learned men, for whose learning and erudition I have such genuine respect, fail to recognize the existence of any real substance at all, of any underlying problem of any Word in the words?

" Do they not see that it is their students' future in the church which lies at the root of the whole matter and which cannot be dismissed as though it were a matter for ' pastoral theology ' ? I myself know what it means year in and year out to mount the steps of the pulpit, conscious of the responsibility to understand and to interpret, and longing to fulfill it, and yet utterly incapable because at the university I had never been brought beyond that well-known ' Awe in the presence of History ' which means in the end that all hope of engaging in the dignity of understanding and interpretation had been surrendered." (Pp. 6–9.)

2. Noncontextual Literalism

We must now ask why the commentator stops short of serious interpretation. For he can scarcely be unaware of the fact that his disconnected notes and comments do not constitute the subject matter of vital communication. If he has ever ministered to a congregation, he will know that their spiritual life is not nourished on such material. What, therefore, does he expect of the preacher or the teacher? The probable answer is that with the use of his notes and comments he expects them to read the meaning straight off from the text. Assuming that they have average qualifications and access to suitable references, they should be able to find the interpretation for themselves. In this respect, and in spite of his approach, the commentator is more of a literalist than he recognizes. At least the confidence that he can leave as serious a task as interpretation to the reader with only a limited number of aids is literalistic in its intention.[18]

What this means is that all considerations of context are relatively unimportant. For if it is possible to read off the meaning from the text directly, and to assume that it constitutes the essential meaning which will not be modified by what the context may further supply, the context can be ignored. At most it will only supply incidental shades of meaning which will make no practical difference to the interpretation. And should this limited approach to the context be of an analytical nature, it will amount to the same emphasis on disconnected notes and comments as before, with the result that the whole quality of the context — its function as a field of relationships — will be further nullified.

The main implication of this refined literalism, which like all literalism is a form of noncontextual thinking, is that it ignores the real life of the people. This follows from the fact that the context of a Biblical passage is not exclusively literary in character, as represented by the chapter and book from which the passage is selected, but cultural and at the same time political and economic, thus providing the background which often makes the greatest difference in the interpretation. Back of every text is the everyday life of the people — that life which is the historical matrix of the text regardless of whether the text is its product or a judgment upon it. For no matter how much we may think of the message of the text as coming from beyond, it is essentially related to the humanity of the Bible and of its writers and Lord.

When, however, we speak of the real life of the people as the decisive context of Biblical interpretation, what do we mean? How shall we define it? By a trial-and-error procedure which adds one unit to another until at length we have enough to satisfy us? By a probe into their private life which aims to uncover a secret substratum of desire? Our answer can only be in terms of those securities which symbolize what people value most, including all those significant human relationships which contribute to them. If we wish a term that gathers the meaning up into itself, we can scarcely do better than to select the modern term " ideology." The real life of the people is equivalent to their ideology — which means their everyday value system, the things they cherish most, which motivate them in their work and play, in their thought and belief, and which above everything else determine their pattern of life and decision.

This observation indicates that the refined literalism of the commentaries like all literalism ignores ideological considerations. The implicit assumption in its approach to the Bible is that the ideology of the ancient people of Palestine is the same as that of any modern people into whose language the Bible is translated. It is the assumption that the grammars and lexicons are equal to the task of translating the one language into the other, as if the task consisted of the translation of units of meaning in comparison to which the ideological context did not matter because it was the same. In recent times, however, we have learned enough of the nature of an ideology to realize how pervasive and subtle and determinative it can be and how, as a way of life, it can shape the thought and behavior of a nation or civilization. We have learned how much it contributes to the meaning of language, especially in those areas which involve human relationships. Depending on one's ideological camp, the same words — democracy, freedom, justice, peace — may have quite opposite meanings, which are not caught up into the word itself in capsule form to be stated in a phrase or two in a lexicon, but which are wider in connotation because they possess the whole quality that derives from the ideology. The members of the opposite ideological camps, although using the same words, may find it next to impossible to understand one another, and either talk past one another or engage in arguments which only end in frayed tempers with no prospect of settlement. A large part of the problem of communication that has troubled the conscience of the church in recent years has arisen from its failure to take the ideological question seriously. Its tradition of literalism, both of the naïve and refined varieties, has proceeded on the assumption that the ideological question did not matter, if, in fact, it was conscious of the question at all. Everyone should be able to understand the Bible merely by virtue of the fact that it was translated into his language — no interpretation that would take into consideration the question of ideological differences as an extension of the task of translation has been considered necessary. "The Bible says" has been considered a sufficient guarantee of successful communication.[19]

As an illustration of what happens when the ideological context of a passage of Scripture is ignored because the reader insists on ascertaining its meaning exclusively from the text, we need only recall the moralistic transformation of the good Samaritan into a respectable middle-class humanitarian whose ideas of goodness are more determined by the mores of Western culture than by the New Testament ethic of grace. In this case the message of the parable is unconsciously adapted to the ideology of Western culture, instead of challenging that ideology as it did the Jewish scribe. For if we depend on the text exclusively, with no knowledge of the ideological context, we may readily conceive of the Samaritan as a moral hero whose example puts the calloused piety of the priest and Levite to shame. We may even be encouraged on this basis to exalt morality over religion. But if we look at the Samaritan in full knowledge of the bad relationship which existed between his people and the Jews, which is a question of ideology, we will see at once that Jesus was selecting an outsider, an alien, a mongrel character, as an example to the scribe, who as an expert in the Jewish law and therefore highly moral in his outlook would undoubtedly be offended. It is as if Jesus had selected a man of a despised race, of an objectionable religious or political order, to set before us, so that, instead of making a hero out of him, his example might put us to shame. For we

must remember that the Samaritan would be one whose people
were despised by the Jews, who were excluded from the Temple, cursed daily in the synagogues with a prayer that peti-
tioned God to deny them eternal salvation, whose testimony
would be inadmissible in a Jewish court of law, and whose
land, for the more pious Jew, was a source of spiritual pollu-
tion to be avoided on journeys northward.[20] In this respect the
selection of the Samaritan as the chief figure in the parable is
a perfect illustration of the Pauline text, " God hath chosen the
foolish things of the world to confound the wise; . . . base
things . . . and things which are despised . . . : that no flesh
should glory in his presence " (I Cor. 1:27-29). And when,
moreover, the radical love of the Samaritan is set in contrast
with the calloused conduct of the most highly respected Jewish religious leaders — the priest and Levite — the offense is
greatly intensified.

The literalistic interpretation read off directly from the text
obscures this offensive role of the Samaritan as the outsider who
knew more of the love of his neighbor than the insider. The
result is that the insiders in the average congregation think it
relatively easy to be good Samaritans by a few acts of conventional charity, and often do not even see that the radical nature
of the Samaritan's love is indicative of an ultimate concern
which shatters and transcends all ordinary love.

3. *Differential Interpretation*

Such an emphasis upon the importance of the context with
special attention to the ideological situation presupposes a relational conception of truth. It means that the Word of God is
known only in relation to real life, which, according to our
definition, and in New Testament terminology, means only in
relation to the flesh. Its ultimate and normative form is the
Word of God incarnate, in which God as truth became known

in the giving of himself. In this respect the discovery of truth and the communication of truth are integral.

On the basis of such a conception it is possible to work out certain principles of interpretation which may be generally described as relational hermeneutics but which, as we shall see, even within this classification are distinguished by an emphasis on significant differences. Our first step in this direction is to claim that the truth of the Bible is known only in conflict — a claim that will be more clearly recognized from the nature of an ideology which, with some qualifications, is, or easily becomes, the politico-sociological equivalent of the religious concept of idolatry, and which bears a striking resemblance to the Pauline understanding of a confidence in the flesh. Conflict is implicit in the fact that an ideology like an idolatry is always in some respect competitive in relation to Biblical truth. Here we need only recall how in both the Old and the New Testament idolatry is always understood in this manner, with the emphasis sometimes on the external competitor who is directly and openly opposed to God, and sometimes on the internal competitor who is indirectly and secretly opposed but compelled to present itself as a false substitute. Both aspects are represented in the figure of the Antichrist. Conflict is a predominant theme in the dramatic events of the Gospel story as it threads its way through the various stages of our Lord's ministry to culminate in the crucifixion itself. As its scope broadens and its intensity deepens, involving a greater number and variety of persons, the impression is almost inescapable that it is fundamental to an understanding of all that is happening. The same impression may be derived from the militant character of the early church confronted by a world in need of evangelization, but resistant to the evangel. Conflict in the form of opposition, argument, persecution, heresy was its portion at every stage. In the life of the individual, conflict with God exists in various forms — in the deep opposition of the unbeliever as an enemy of God, and in the peculiar resistance of the believer, who is either tempted or who in honesty is aware of the shadow side of faith. For this reason it is a mistake to think of the competitor as always out there, before our eyes, as a counterclaimant with respect to doctrine and practice and other facets of faith, because this would be too facile. It would not comprehend the personal aspect of faith, the deep hidden and inward dimension according to which, from the opposite side, the real competitor is God himself, as he competes for our love and devotion against our hearts themselves, which are so often persuaded that he is an alien power and not the one who loves with an everlasting love. Not to recognize this dimension of faith as the struggle of the soul with God, who in his never-ceasing search for the lost follows us all the way to bring us back to the fold, would be blindness. For it concerns the center of our conception.

This should indicate that the claim concerning Biblical truth only known in conflict has to be qualified in such a manner that it is not thought to refer to any kind of conflict. For it is obvious that there are many forms of conflict that involve no possibility of revelation and which are only worthy of condemnation. A misguided zeal to defend the faith, or a shallow contentious spirit which always leaves its legacy of trouble, never brings us to a knowledge of the truth. Fanaticism in any form is often a defense against that decisive conflict which, if entered upon, would only mean its defeat.

It is now appropriate to ask how these observations pertain to the interpretation of Scripture. If Biblical truth is known only in conflict, how will this affect our hermeneutical principles? The answer that at this stage seems most consistent and constructive is one that emphasizes the necessity of always ascertaining what stands over against the main thrust of meaning in any passage of Scripture, in a relation of opposition to it. It is the practice of always ascertaining the identity of the competitor — be it a person, institution, doctrine, power, or other factor within the scope of the ideology, which would negate the God of the Bible as he may be revealed or represented.

The advantage of such a practice, in contrast to that of beginning and ending with a quantum of Biblical truth which remains unrelated to the ideological situation, is its dynamic character which, for the purpose of communication, has a greater possibility of involving the hearer. It means an end to the conventional practice of interpreting the Bible as a thing of itself without informing the hearer of what stands over against it at every stage. For how is it possible to have an adequate understanding of the Christian faith if one is never permitted to understand with equal clarity what opposes it? If one may illustrate from the book of The Acts, how is it possible to understand the experience of the early church if one is not provided with an adequate knowledge of the Jewish Temple cult, of the Judaizing party within the church, and of the various forms of Gentile paganism, including Caesar worship? It is obvious, of course, that this is what seldom happens in the pulpit, church school, and perhaps even in the theological seminary. The competitors of the Christian faith, in the interests of safety, are never permitted to appear in visible form, even though in actual life they are often more than visible. The people hear and see the preacher expounding a passage from the book of The Acts. They see how earnest he is, how excited he becomes, how he thumbs the pages of this presumably important book, and they gather that there must be something over against the Biblical message, in opposition to it. But they fail to discover what it is because he never really tells them. His action to them is not unlike that of a pugilist in a ring pounding his opponent but his opponent always remaining invisible to the spectators.

The next step in our statement of principles is that of recognizing what is implicit in the conception of truth known only in conflict, in which the identity and character of the competitor is always established as a matter of hermeneutical practice. It is the claim that difference must have priority over similarity. What this means in practice is that the truth of a Biblical passage is more likely to be found at the point of difference between the fundamental thrust of its message and the competitor over against it, than at the point of similarity where there is no possibility of conflict between them. Or, to put it in another way, the truth of a passage is more likely to be found along the boundary line of difference that distinguishes the message from the situation to which it is addressed. The reason for such a claim, if we wish to comment on its ultimate validation, is that it derives from two considerations — the first of which is the transcendence of God, according to which he is essentially different from the created order, and the second of which is the sinfulness of man, according to which he imposes a difference of his own which is alien to himself and God. Any similarity between God and man is relative to both types of difference. These observations apply all along the line that distinguishes Israel from the nations, the church from the world, the new man from the old man, and the Word of God from the word of man — that mysterious line that runs through both the Old and the New Testament in relation to which their content derives its significance. What we are saying is that a knowledge of the truth is primarily acquired by involvement in difference — by a confrontation of the holiness of God and of human sinfulness — and that all truth known by involvement in similarity ultimately derives its meaning from it and is relative to it. As a consequence it must be pointed out that a knowledge of truth obtained in this manner will always involve one in suffering and will appear as something alien.

It would be a serious error, however, to minimize the importance of the factor of similarity, because similarity is necessary for the issuance of any difference in conflict. It is the factor that holds the differences closely enough together to make the conflict possible, like the field of battle which provides the common ground for the opposing sides to meet each other. In the case of the early church and the Temple cult, it was the fact that they were both so Jewish that made their differences so sharp, and in the case of the early church and the Judaizers, the fact that they were not only both so Jewish but both so Christian. If we apply the same observation to Christ, it is because he is so human that the difference that separates us from him offends. If we apply it to hermeneutics, it is because of what the interpreter has in common with the hearer that the difference he espouses disturbs the hearer and communicates the truth. When the interpreter has nothing in common with the hearer, or on the other hand, everything in common, he fails to communicate.

But is this not an admission that the factor of similarity has a priority? For how is it possible to advance the idea of a common ground without implying that differences are adjustable to it and therefore capable of being resolved. To this, one would have to reply that to some extent it may be an admission, but that the purpose other than this is the recognition of the historical and the human as the locus of conflict, and therefore the locus of various kinds of differences, some of which are superficial and temporary and therefore amenable to a common ground, but others of which are not amenable and as such are the object of our discussion. These latter are of two principal types: first, historical differences at the level of human relations which, in defiance of rational treatment, resist the problem-solving technique and which in appearance at least involve genuinely incompatible factors; and secondly, transcendental differences, which are hidden within these historical differences, but which in principle are irreducible, and which bear no direct or continuous relationship with any ground of similarity. As an illustration of the former, one might select any sharp boundary line of difference of an ideological character; and of the latter, the difference that separates God and man. Our claim, as far as hermeneutics is concerned, is that one is more likely to find the truth of the Bible in the area of these latter differences than in the area of the common ground whose relation to them is by no means obvious.

To some extent the old figure of the baited hook may clarify what we mean by the priority of difference to similarity where it is a question of the transcendental. In this case similarity is the bait within which the fundamental difference is concealed. As we bite on the similarity we find ourselves hooked by the fundamental difference. When this happens there is no doubt about the priority of the hook to the bait. It is the hook with which we have to reckon. If now we think of the incarnation, we will recognize how Christological such a hermeneutical principle can be. The flesh of Christ is representative of the similarity that obtains between us and him, while the Word is representative of the difference. As we feed on his flesh it becomes the bait by means of which we are caught by the Word. If we seem to have exploited the illustration, it will suffice to indicate our desire to ground our hermeneutics in Christology.

The natural question to ask the Biblical interpreter who wishes to hold fast to the priority of differences is what his task should be when confronted by the transcendental. Is it enough to remain open to it as a possibility, but one that is not immediately significant? Or is it to be affirmed with the directness appropriate only to a visible object? Or is it to be affirmed only indirectly, as a factor to which he can only point? Or is there another possibility suggested by the role of the witness, which has the advantage of not implying the static nature of something to which one can only point?

If none of these alternatives seems desirable, it is because they imply a degree of familiarity with the transcendental that is less than genuine, and which for this reason suggests that the interpreter has been up against, not the transcendental, but a symbolical form of it. For if he explores the differences as the main thrust of his task, he will increasingly incur a greater risk of offense as the possibility of an irreducible difference confronts him. This will be accentuated by the fact that the presupposition of an affinity, which is taken for granted in all varieties of hermeneutics influenced by the philosophy of idealism, is called into question, or at least strained to the breaking point. The difference will be so acute that no similarity will be adequate as its explanation. The interpreter will not be able to preserve the equanimity of a mind that is presumed to be open, or to point, or even to witness, in the conventional manner in which this is usually understood, but will more likely resist, ignore, or even deny it, as will be better understood when it is realized how alien is the truth that now confronts him. Nor is the dimension of his difficulty reduced if he stands within the context of faith, because faith is not of such a nature that it allows him to recover from the offense and leave it behind as something that, for a time, was merely an unfortunate misunderstanding of unbelief. For the man of faith is offended, and continues to be offended, not only as a man of faith but as an interpreter, because the cross is never lightened. In evangelical language, he must continue to bear about in his body the dying of the Lord Jesus. He is never able to recover from the uniqueness of that which confronts him. It is always something that shatters his natural preference for similarity, analogy, human language, and community, to which he holds with all the persistence he can muster, because in these things his ideology is grounded. Under these circumstances he inevitably suffers. If he is honest enough with what confronts him, his most adequate response will be a confession of the offense, which, as a form of witness, will correspond to the alien form of the truth.

4. *Illustration of Principles*

It would be unwise to leave our discussion at too abstract a level without attempting to illustrate its adaptation to a portion of Scripture, and to suggest how the hermeneutical principles apply. For this purpose we select the book of The Acts in the hope that by seeing it within its ancient ideological context its relevance for the modern reader may be heightened, and that the odds and ends of knowledge into which it is often fragmented may begin to fall into place. This, of course, is only another way of saying that the book ought to be respected as a book. For it is all very well to turn to the book for interesting studies of ecclesiastical precedent, conversions, and religious success stories, but this in the last analysis is often indicative of a refusal to become involved in the ideological issues that made the book what it is and that constitute its *raison d'être*.

We proceed within a frame of reference indicated by B in relation to C, where B represents the book of The Acts and C the competitor, with *r* the relation of difference between them. Since differences are more frequently expressed historically in the form of ideological conflict, the first step is to look for major indications of such a fact.

When we do this, we find that the book concerns the crossing of that strange line which was partly religious, partly racial, and partly geographical, dividing the Jewish from the

Gentile world, the crossing of which, or more correctly the obliteration of which, was attended by conflict, inward and outward, an event that at the same time was a manifestation of the catholicity of the church. The Acts is the story of how this happened, first in conflict with the Temple cult at Jerusalem, then with the Judaizers within the church, finally with Gentile paganism. The structure of the book is controlled by these three conflicts. The first part is set in Palestine with its typical Jewish atmosphere and the Temple cult as the predominant institution; the second is the Gentile world with its typical Hellenistic atmosphere, in which synagogues and pagan temples are predominant. Somewhere on the line that divides the two, occupying as it were the midsection of the book, is the story of the internal conflict within the church itself, involving the Judaizers and culminating in the Great Council.

A study of these three conflicts is a most effective means of grasping what the book is saying, because it begins as a matter of hermeneutical principle with the ideological issues that were the most dynamic and meaningful to the writer and his contemporaries. In each case the identity of B and the competitor C is as obvious as the relation r which defines the conflict between them. Since the competitor must be taken seriously, it means that a serious study of the Jewish Temple cult, the Judaizers, and the various forms of Gentile paganism is essential to a study of The Acts. What each had in common with the early church is equally essential for an understanding of what divided them.

The main consideration is that the more accurately we establish the nature of the fundamental difference implicit in the relation of conflict r in any given case, the more accurately we can establish its parallel in any modern situation. The modern parallel of the ancient Temple cult may be any form of institutional religion that presumes to have a monopoly of the presence of God and that, for this reason, substitutes loyalty to itself for loyalty to him. The modern parallel of the Judaizers may be anyone with an equivalent claim, who, instead of urging that it is first necessary to Judaize in order to Christianize, substitutes his own culture for Judaism and says that it is first necessary to Westernize, Aryanize, Anglicize, Americanize, or Orientalize in order to Christianize, as the case may be. The modern parallel to Gentile paganism may be any cult of the state if we are thinking of the Roman imperial cult, or any worship of natural vitality if we are thinking of the earth-mother goddesses.

In each case of a parallel involving a modern ideological issue, the interpreter moves into an area where the offense of the Biblical message will involve him in a risk, particularly if it pertains to his own way of life. It will involve him in suffering, particularly if he sees the truth of the Biblical message as alien to a system of values that he has always held sacred and which has symbolized his securities. For in this respect it will not be alien merely to vague generalities such as sin, secularism, materialism, and the like, which as examples of irresponsible simplification permit him to escape the offense, but to things which he has previously regarded as good, and indeed of the highest value. It will strike at all the contemporary equivalents of the Pauline confidence in the flesh " circumcised on the eighth day, of the people of Israel, of the tribe of Benjamin, a Hebrew born of Hebrews; as to the law a Pharisee, as to zeal a persecutor of the church, as to righteousness under the law blameless."

The most decisive aspect of the problem will emerge when he attempts to move into the center of each area of conflict to ascertain the source of the offense, if possible in terms of the transcendental dimension. The questions pertinent to such an undertaking will have to do with the dynamic source of the

Christian faith as a historical movement. Why, for example, was it able to obliterate the rigid line between the Jewish and Gentile worlds? Why was it able to dissolve the wall of partition between them? Why was it able to work its way from Jerusalem to Rome in a single generation, from synagogue to synagogue, from city to city, against opposition and frequent persecution? Why its persistence, its sense of mission, its intolerance of its competitors? What was its secret? Questions of this nature must be asked at every stage to understand the deeper difference which symbolized its power.

Facile answers which evade the ideological context will be inadequate no matter how much they appeal to the Holy Spirit, on the ground that the acts of the apostles were at the same time the acts of the Spirit. Such an appeal will be correct in its intention but not in its understanding of the Spirit, because the Spirit is known not in abstraction but historically in relation to real life. The presence of the Holy Spirit as the secret of the mission and message of the church, if we may be guided by the incidents in The Acts, is always particularized, always oriented toward the real life of man where his sin is most effectively concealed, where under the guise of an ideological goodness the real sin of his civilization is most dangerously operative. This does not mean that the early church was anti-Semitic or anti-Hellenistic, any more than the modern church is anti-Western or anti-Eastern, but that what the modern church has to do is to save the Westerner from his way of life as it does the Easterner from his, in order that both may be one in Christ.

As the interpreter moves into the center of this gospel of Christ for us, it means, so far as The Acts is concerned, that he moves into the center of its kerygmatic content. In other words, the movement which began with historical interpretation and which by nature is didactic and as such comprises the greater part of The Acts, ends with the kerygma and what it signifies. The movement is from teaching to preaching. This agrees, of course, with the obvious fact that for the writer of The Acts the historical interpretation is the ideological matrix of the sermons of the apostles. We cannot separate the sermonic material out of the historical interpretation without losing something in the process. For what happened in the life and work of the church as the subject matter of interpretation is really an indirect form of the kerygma. The historical interpretation is not unlike the flesh of the incarnate Christ in which the Word is found. But the bare word cannot be extracted from it. Therefore any list of the elements of the kerygma extracted from the book of The Acts, however valuable for scholarly research, must not deceive us into thinking that such a method should determine our hermeneutics. For it encourages the rather erroneous idea that the gospel can be preached by a recital of the bare elements of the kerygma without the historical matrix integral to it, which is the old noncontextual positivism again with its self-contained units of truth.

5 | The Unity of Preaching and Teaching

1. *The Nature of the Problem*

As we now shift our attention to the first century and to the crucial question of whether the New Testament subordinates the teaching ministry, our main consideration will be that the prevailing disposition of recent years has been to answer it in the affirmative. The conception that has largely succeeded in capturing the field and commending itself as one of the conspicuous features of New Testament study of the past few decades has been that the apostolic church undoubtedly assumed that only after the gospel had been proclaimed and believed could teaching properly begin. Preaching was therefore prior to teaching and created the condition on which teaching was possible and meaningful. Preaching was primarily intended for the evangelization of those outside the church, while teaching was intended for the edification of those inside the church. Between the two a line of distinction was always more or less sharply drawn. Preaching referred to the proclamation of the message of the promised Messiah who had come and fulfilled his mission, who had been crucified and raised from the dead, and who would return to judge the world (kerygma). It had nothing to do with the conventional conception of a moralistic exhortation.[21]

This widely accepted representation of the New Testament

conception of preaching and teaching fails, however, to do justice to the unity that, on Biblical grounds, ought to obtain between them. For no matter how much the sharpness of the distinction may be modified, this does not of itself provide an answer to the complexity of the relationship that binds them together. This weakness, which is largely an oversimplification of the problem due to an excessive dependence on documentary definitions, is most conspicuous in the kind of purism that frequently emerges at the level of its popularization. Here it is often presumed that the distinction between preaching and teaching is largely a matter of differing forms of literary content. Preaching is regarded as merely the communication of the elements of the kerygma as recovered by research; teaching is merely the doctrine and ethics which interpret the kerygma. Similarily with preaching as intended for those outside the church and teaching for those inside — the distinction is frequently applied in the crassest manner, forgetting that the believer is often one who has to struggle against his own unbelief (Mark 9:24), and therefore needs to hear the gospel repeatedly, albeit in new and creative forms, and that the unbeliever is often one who is attracted by a penetrating interpretation of the Christian faith in depth.

The other weakness, which is more serious in character, is that the sharper the separation of preaching from teaching, the more it encourages a reliance on some alleged variety of direct revelation. This is always consonant with the fact that the church is tempted by the deceptive possibility of a " pure " form of preaching uncontaminated by the preacher — which in this case would have to do with the human means by which he interprets and communicates his message (teaching). On the one side is this " pure " preaching — " pure " because of the supposed directness with which it relates to God and to the people — involving perhaps a variety of things: a mystical apprehension, a noumenal awareness, an emotional resurgence, an existential encounter, and eschatological confrontation; any one, or a combination of them, is capable of reinforcing the assumption that the essential meaning of the Bible can be read directly off from the text, and therefore dispensing with the necessity of serious interpretation (teaching). On the other side is teaching which, separated off from this " pure " form of preaching, and with little recognition given to its essential character as human language and communication, is regarded as of secondary importance, and perhaps only as a subsequent rationalization. We should not assume, however, that in any specific representation of the conception in question the line between preaching and teaching is ever drawn as sharply as this. We have overemphasized it for the purpose of showing as clearly as possible what the weakness tends to be. But even with this concession and the utmost that can be said for it, the problem remains. For inasmuch as justice has not been done to the essential unity between preaching and teaching, the implicit encouragement this gives to a conception of direct revelation cannot but remain. What we are saying in effect is that the relatively sharp distinction between kerygma (gospel) and didache (teaching) tends to conceal within itself a relatively sharp distinction between revelation and reason, eschatology and history, grace and truth, religious experience and didactic content, according to which, in practice, what is on either side of the distinction would seem to be accessible in a surprisingly pure form, with the priority always given the former over the latter.

In dealing with this problem it is advisable to recognize, if only in a tentative manner, that the primary distinction between preaching and teaching is that preaching stands closer to revelation while teaching stands closer to reason. These cannot be separated as though relevation could come first in a positive purity, and directness followed by reason as its interpretation. And this holds whether revelation be regarded as mystical, existential, or eschatological, or a combination of all. Much as Christ emphasized the essential mystery of revelation which no amount of didactic skill can ever compel, he never ignored the humanity of the hearer by assuming that revelation could occur in any context other than real life, and in those situations where basic questions are raised and men compelled to think for themselves. Consequently, what has to be recognized is the unity that is involved between revelation and reason, and therefore between preaching and teaching. The crucial question is how this unity should be understood. The answer that provides, as it were, the key to the ensuing discussion is that whereas preaching has reference to God making himself known through and in spite of the preacher to the heart of the believer, teaching has reference to the interpretation and communication of the message by human means. Both are inseparably united in one act, in that the Word of God is heard through the word of man. That is to say, preaching is to teaching what the Word of God is to the word of man. In this respect, the unity of the one word with the other is not unlike the unity of the incarnation, in which the Word of God became flesh, and this, in a manner that no one was able to hear the Word apart from the flesh, but through the flesh and with due regard for the flesh. " Every spirit that confesseth that Jesus Christ is come in the flesh is of God." (I John 4:2.) Our main point is that the same regard for the flesh holds good for preaching. Hearing the word of God (revelation) will always involve a high regard for the flesh, which is but the teaching element integral to preaching.

2. Transcendence and Arbitrariness

One of the indications that some conception of direct revelation is influencing the preacher is that a certain arbitrariness creeps into his preaching. It is not the humble certainty of the prophet or the apostle, which as a sign of strength enabled him to stand even before a persecutor with a disarming boldness. It is rather the authoritarian spirit of which the psychologists speak, and which suggests the authority of coercive power imputed by man to God. This is not too much to claim, considering the manner in which it impels the preacher to parade the facts and events of the gospel (kerygma) as if self-evident to the hearer — to announce, proclaim, and declare them as if their truth, for no other reason than his manner of speaking, should immediately be revealed.

Such arbitrariness involves, of course, a serious disregard for the humanity of the hearer, because for him the facts and events are not self-evident. He cannot read their meaning off directly as the preacher presumes he can. He is a man with many limitations of ability, opportunity, and growth. The sacred, somewhat professional vocabulary which is integral to preaching escapes him. He needs interpretation (teaching), which is integral to the act of preaching, not because he is a sinner — which, of course, he is — but because he is a human being. He needs it not primarily as a sign of the intelligibility of the gospel — important as this is — but as a sign of the preacher's love for him.

If preaching by its nature stands closer to revelation, according to a Biblical understanding of the term, this will suggest the qualifications of the genuine preacher and how he differs from his arbitrary counterpart. At the same time, it will suggest why preaching is still of primary importance despite all that has been said of the value of teaching and of the danger of subordinating it. First and most obviously, he will not presume to have access to a form of direct revelation, nor act as if he had an encyclopedic knowledge of God, both of which would sufficiently convince him of being such a strong man of faith in comparison with his people that he would have a right to speak by virtue of it. That is to say, he will not presume to have criteria of revelation other than the self-validating Lord himself, nor resort to alleged proofs of God in the hope of prying the unbeliever out of his entrenched position. He will be an essentially humble man, which means that he is not a slave of authoritarianism — humble because he has no direct revelation, only the suffering, dying, and risen Lord who is an offense to all directness; humble, moreover, because he is a sinner as the servants of God know so well. Therefore he will be puzzled to know why he was ever called to be a preacher and what right of himself he has to speak more than those to whom he speaks. To use the figure of the Old Testament, he will be a suffering servant — suffering not only because he identifies himself with those who are against God in their sin and alienated from themselves and others, but because he comes not with excellency of speech and (worldly) wisdom, but in weakness, in fear, and in much trembling, determined to know nothing among his people but Jesus Christ and him crucified (I Cor. 2:1-3). He will strain the richest and best interpretation (teaching) of the Bible and of life to its breaking point, because being a man and able to use nothing other than human language, he will never avoid being a teacher, even though he stands under revelation. Although a teacher by the sheer fact that he is obliged to use human language, he will as a preacher break through this language. His communication will be in a broken language, which is essentially the language of the preacher, not of the teacher — broken as the Suffering Servant is broken and therefore capable of a vicarious communication unknown to the teacher. At the same time he will have an assurance that goes beyond the assurance of the intelligible, reaching into the mystery content of the Bible in its deepest significance: " O the depth of the riches both of the wisdom and knowledge of God! how unsearchable are his judgments, and his ways past finding out! " (Rom. 11:33). His joy and hope will be equally strange because they will be neither the extension of natural optimism, nor the facile confidence which presupposes its own security, nor the blind credulity which lives in a fool's paradise. They will face all the sorrow, tragedy, and darkness of the world and not succumb: " Although the fig tree shall not blossom, neither shall fruit be in the vines; the labor of the olive shall fail, and the fields shall yield no meat; the flock shall be cut off from the fold, and there shall be no herd in the stalls: yet I will rejoice in the Lord, I will joy in the God of my salvation " (Hab. 3:17-18).

Because the preacher stands in this respect under revelation, his task possesses a genuine priority over that of the teacher — genuine in its transcendental dimension, which means that when he comes to know God, God does not hand himself over to him and thus permit him to possess him as the teacher possesses knowledge and wisdom. Our protest against the subordination of the teaching ministry is at the same time an indirect protest against the kind of preaching that has perverted its understanding of such priority into an arbitrariness — in brief, the kind of preaching that has presumed to equate the transcendental with the arbitrary. For why should one assume that human arbitrariness should ever be representative of the evangelical understanding of the transcendental? Why should the arbitrariness of the preacher in proclaiming Christ be considered more truly representative of the Word of God incarnate than other forms of communication? Why should authoritarianism have anything to do with revelation? One of the secondary motives behind this association of the transcendental with the arbitrary has been the reaction against the rational as a possible *praeparatio evangelica*. The preacher has thought that his peremptory pronouncement of the facts and proclamation of the events, without regard to the humanity of the hearer, would somehow keep in his place the teacher whose proclivity toward the rational arouses the suspicion that underneath his knowledge and wisdom lurks a *praeparatio evangelica*. Our main concern — much as we recognize the danger of the latter — is to emphasize that the presupposition underlying the arbitrariness of the preacher is only another variety of the same thing. Moreover, an earlier chapter would indicate that it is not the fear of a *praeparatio evangelica* that is the real explanation of the arbitrariness, but the fear of the intelligible as a mediation of the offense. For, unless we are mistaken, the arbitrariness of the pulpit is a sign that the offense has been eliminated from it. When this has happened, it is easy to assume that the oratorical compulsion of saying things " out of the blue " is equivalent to the breaking in of the word of God.

One of the more problematical forms of arbitrariness remains, however, to be considered — the tendency of attributing to the facts and events of the gospel a greater purity and authority than is warranted by Scriptural evidence. This tendency undoubtedly appeals to a certain desire to absolutize the facts and events and to invest them with a kind of scientific demonstrability that goes beyond their nature as testimony. In spirit it is the same positivism that characterizes the modern world with its worship of the scientific, and which in the pulpit enables the preacher to sound all the more authoritative. But, for all its accentuation of the factual and the chronological, it does not ring true to the New Testament, because the apostles were not conscious of preaching facts and events as such, but of preaching Christ. They were so conscious of his presence that even when they particularized his mighty acts as things seen and heard, they could not speak with the detachment of scientists, but as those personally committed to his service. Since the Lord from beyond (transcendent) was in their midst, they did not need to endow the facts and events with a greater authority than was warranted. His presence provided an authentication which rendered this unnecessary. His presence, which might be regarded as the evangelical version of the transcendental, prevented the facts and events from being endowed with an authority which belonged only to the transcendental.

We stress this point because the recent habit of characterizing preaching as a proclamation of facts and events tends to encourage this error.[22] The authority that belongs only to the transcendental tends to be transferred to them under the guise of positivism, which means that the priority of the transcendental is also transferred. As a result, the evangelical perspective is seriously altered. The preacher is tempted to speak of the facts and events as if they were equivalent to direct revelation, and therefore to forget the authentication that comes of the presence of his Lord. No longer does he look upon the priority of preaching as the genuine priority of the transcendental, but as the priority of the factual to the interpretive, or of the eventful to the interpretive. In other words, the genuine priority of the transcendental has been illegitimately transformed into both a logical and a chronological priority. The result can only be an assertion of the authoritarian spirit.

3. *An Argument for Unity*

Our insistence upon the unity of preaching and teaching as the primary consideration within which the transcendental priority of preaching can be preserved and understood has not been for any other purpose than that each should fulfill its highest purpose in the service of Christ and his church. It has not been for the purpose of carving out the largest portion possible for the teaching ministry, because this would only be a perversion of preaching from the opposite side. It has been as much for the safeguarding of the best interests of preaching as it has been for those of teaching, because both stand or fall together. Where the teaching ministry is subordinated it can only mean that the preaching ministry has been perverted as a complementary aspect of the process. Where the one is not taken seriously it means that the other is not taken seriously, except that in the one case the evidence of such indifference may be more obvious than in the other. In its essential nature the preservation of the unity of preaching and teaching is the same as the preservation of the unity of grace and truth, inasmuch as the kerygma is representative of the grace of God and the didache representative of the truth of God. Furthermore, it is the same as the preservation of the unity of the gospel and law, which is the task of recognizing where and why they are one and the same — a task to which reformed theology has been especially devoted.

The fact that teaching is integral to preaching ought to be evident from the fact that tradition is integral to revelation. The word of God is heard through the medium of the terminology, thought forms, and perspective of a given period of history. It is particularized with respect to place and time and indirectly communicated by means of a particularized tradition. This tradition as tradition is communicated as any other didactic material is communicated — subject to all the peculiarities and limitations of human agencies. This fact has undoubtedly been emphasized of late by the Bultmann controversy. For any thought that the significance of the facts and events of the gospel message could be read off directly by the modern man, as the arbitrariness of the pulpit so often suggests by its proclamatory manner, has been thoroughly dispelled. It can only be grasped when, among other conditions, it has been made relevant for him by means of interpretation. In other words, what Bultmann is saying is that preaching is only possible in so far as it includes teaching — a special form of teaching, one devoted to the task of making the content of the gospel more relevant. If anything, the Bultmann controversy is symptomatic of a crisis in the teaching ministry, of what happens to preaching when the teaching which should have been integral to it has been subordinated.

But if we judge correctly, teaching was regarded as integral to the gospel from the earliest times, not as something that could be described as previous or subsequent to its proclamation, but as something so intimately involved in it that any logical or chronological distinctions were impossible. It so enveloped the proclamation with a fleshly, historical form that the word of God was only heard out of its midst as the word from beyond, regardless of the particularity of the facts and events involved. That is to say, the gospel was at once a reinterpretation (teaching) of an already existent tradition which was mainly Old Testament in content, supplemented by contemporary Jewish religion and practice, including apocalypticism. This tradition, for the most part, constituted the atmosphere, substance, and language by means of which the gospel was communicated. Whereas the Christ event was unique and discrete, it was never so completely particularized that its relationship with the past was forgotten. Instead, it was always proclaimed upon the background of the past, as an event that both interpreted the past and was in turn interpreted by it. In order to preach the gospel, the apostles and the evangelists invariably expounded the Old Testament. They could not think of a form of preaching that was so particularized that it was not brought under the discipline of Old Testament interpretation, and particularly that of prophetic anticipation of the coming of the Messiah — all of which was signified by the familiar Pauline phrase " according to the Scriptures."

It was the same with Christ himself. His allusions to his identity, according to the Gospel of John, were embodied in a reinterpretation of the Old Testament, focusing upon the high points of its history as represented in the great religious festivals. He was the bread from heaven (ch. 6:50), the light of the world (ch. 8:12), the shepherd of Israel (ch. 10:11,16), the passover lamb (ch. 19:14), with each metaphor involving at the same time both interpretation (teaching) and testimony (preaching). In this double-sidedness of the Christ who came into the midst of his people both as one who was known (historical) and yet unknown (eternal), we have the unity of the word and flesh which provides the key to a proper understanding of the unity of preaching and teaching. His preaching (testimony) and teaching (interpretation) were inseparable. His divine word could not be heard independently of his human speech, any more than his human speech could be heard independently of his divine word.[23] Those who tried to hear his speech only as human speech could only conclude that it was a testimony of himself which, according to most standards, seemed but the ultimate in egotism, if not a form of madness (John 8:13;10:20). Others who heard in it the divine word came to a completely opposite conclusion and confessed him as the Promised One (chs. 6:68-69;7:41,46).

These observations on the incarnate unity of Christ's divine word and human speech provide the most likely explanation of certain texts in the Pauline epistles which have reference to the nature of the gospel on the one hand as tradition, on the other as revelation, and which provide further evidence in support of the unity of preaching and teaching. In the first epistle to the Corinthians there are those texts which speak of the gospel as received and delivered, and where the use of the technical terms *paralambano* and *paradidomi* indicate that the apostle is thinking of the reception and transmission of a tradition by human means. In this respect the gospel has the connotation of human language and is didactic. It can be taught. But in contrast to these texts, there are others in the Galatian epistle in which Paul insists that he only received the gospel by revelation and he sharply distinguishes this from teaching and other forms of human communication: "The gospel which was preached of me is not after man. For I neither received it of man, neither was I taught it, but by the revelation of Jesus Christ" (Gal. 1:11-12). The question this suggests is why Paul in the Corinthian texts could speak of the gospel as transmissible by human means, but in the Galatian texts say the opposite, in his assertion that it came to him only by revelation. Why such seemingly contradictory statements? The answer will be found if we remember that he thinks of the gospel as having a double aspect. It is both the word of man in the form of tradition, and the word of God in the form of revelation. Consequently he can think of it from the one aspect as being taught, and from the other as not being taught. The importance of this for our discussion is that it implies a unity between the gospel tradition and revelation which is similar to the unity between preaching and teaching.[24] Although when Paul speaks of having received the gospel by revelation he probably means his hearing Christ on the road to Damascus, this does not nullify the fact that others have received it by revelation from the lips of a preacher. This was certainly the case with the Thessalonians, as Paul indicates himself in the familiar text, " For this cause also thank we God without ceasing, because, when ye received the word of God which ye heard of us, ye received it not as the word of men, but as it is in truth, the word of God" (I Thess. 2:13). Thus, there is always a double aspect, the gospel as the word of men which is communicable by human means and therefore taught, and the gospel as the word of God which is not communicable by human means, but revealed. Preaching has reference to the fact that over and above and beyond all human means of communication, and yet out of the midst of it, revelation occurs. The people do hear the word of God from the lips of the preacher. In all this there is always a strange unity of the word of the preacher with the word of God, in spite of the fact that the latter is revealed.

In the Synoptic Gospels, the unity may be observed particularly in the manner in which Matthew and Luke incorporate the teaching of Jesus (didache) into the gospel narrative (kerygma) as if to indicate that the two are integral. Some authorities have played down the significance of this fact on the ground that it betrays a later tendency to rabbinize Jesus, whereas others have attributed it to a desire to preserve his teachings after the immediate hope of the Parousia had begun to wane. But none of these possibilities is adequate to explain the peculiar unity which as a literary and theological problem confronts one in the way in which the teaching of Jesus and the gospel narrative are incorporated into each other. The parables, of course, illustrate this unity, if one may be guided by recent studies which give greater recognition to their evangelical content, even though they were the characteristic form in which Jesus taught.[25] In this respect they qualify as didactic kerygma.[26] But the principal matter in mind is the manner in which Matthew and Luke adopt the gospel material from Mark with its emphasis on the acts of Jesus, and by the incorporation of didactic material accentuate their significance as truth. It suggests, as it were, a fear that an exclusive emphasis on the acts of Jesus might convey the impression that he was a wonder-worker and not one whose action was at the same time an encounter with truth. As a wonder-worker he might very well be regarded as representative of what presumably would be the grace of God — even if it were only magic — and this with no relation to truth, where truth is the offense that confronts men with the reality of their historical situation. The Docetic possibilities of such a representation would be too significant to disregard.

The way in which Matthew and Luke thus succeed in representing Jesus as teacher, which is one of their characteristics in comparison to Mark, is not of such a nature that it could be explained on a literary basis alone. Their treatment of the didactic material, and more especially their revision of the Marcan material, suggests a consciousness of the fact that the problem was spiritual and theological in character, and that it was of such importance as to warrant a thorough reworking of all the material available. A distinguished New Testament scholar speaks of this incorporation of the teaching of Jesus into the heart of the apostolic kerygma, and particularly of the incorporation of the Q source into the Gospels of Matthew and Luke, as perhaps the most important single incident in the history of Christian literature.[27] If this assessment of the achievement of Matthew and Luke is correct, its implication for the unity of preaching and teaching is undoubtedly most significant.

4. *Chronological Priority*

Certain evidence from Pauline sources which seems to establish a chronological priority of preaching to teaching and which therefore has a bearing on the question of their unity remains to be considered. It has reference mainly to the familiar distinction between the babe in Christ and the mature believer and the foundation and the superstructure, where both metaphors signify successive stages of faith. The babe in Christ comes first, followed by the mature believer; the foundation comes first, followed by the superstructure — the first in both cases signifying the hearing of the fundamental content of the gospel as occurs in the initial stage of faith, the second signifying the growth of wisdom, involving teaching which interprets the gospel.

It is commonly held that such wisdom is equivalent to a theological superstructure of thought, consisting of doctrine and ethics, which is built upon the fundamental content of the gospel by means of some sort of additive process. The metaphors are thought of more or less literally, with emphasis on the physical fact of the superstructure erected on the foundation and the physical fact of maturity as a natural growth from infancy. In both cases it is a fairly straightforward conception of adding one thing to another in chronological sequence. The question, however, is, Does Paul conceive of the gospel and wisdom in this manner? Does he think of the one added to the other, as a given content of knowledge may be added to a store of knowledge already possessed?

What persuades us against such a conception is that the wisdom of which Paul speaks is a wisdom imparted by the Holy Spirit. This is important, because it suggests that the wisdom in question is living insight first and theological doctrine second. As it develops into a rich complexity of insight, it forms what may be described as a context of understanding out of which theological thought in its abstract form crystallizes. Consequently, theological thought is always a second stage removed. This is surely supported by the fact that in the church there are many mature believers whose wisdom in specific situations is full of evangelical insight, but who are unlearned as judged by the standards of academic theology. This would be evidently true of the early church as well.

But the wisdom imparted by the Holy Spirit is more. It is a wisdom that is never dissociated from the presence of the Holy Spirit. Where such wisdom is manifested, there is the Holy Spirit. This is the conclusion that follows naturally from Paul's understanding of the indwelling presence of the Spirit and the interiorized fellowship with his own spirit. But in view of the further fact that he holds firmly to a Christological understanding of the Spirit, the presence of the Spirit is at the same time the presence of the living Christ. This is why he speaks somewhat interchangeably of the presence of the Spirit and of the presence of Christ (Rom., ch. 8). The importance of this fact, as far as our interpretation of wisdom is concerned, is that it permits the conclusion that the wisdom is never dissociated from the presence of Christ. Since the presence of Christ means the presence of the kerygma in its primary sense as the living Word of God, this means the wisdom is never dissociated from it. Wisdom as living insight and kerygma as the presence of Christ are contemporaneous.

The wisdom for which Paul pleads to the Corinthians is therefore a wisdom that can come only by their hearing the living Christ afresh in each situation — in the context of each of the several problems which confronted them in the church: the quarreling factions, the lawsuits, the sexual and marital difficulties, the doubtful experiments in Christian liberty, the disorders of worship, and the false conceptions of destiny. That

16712

this interpretation of Paul's conception of wisdom is closer to what he had in mind is confirmed by the Christological orientation of his pastoral counseling (wisdom), as we see from every section of the epistle. It is the insight characteristic of one who knew that Christ repeated, Christ anew in each situation, would be creative of the wisdom so badly needed.

Chronological priority is therefore only a relative distinction applying to the amount of wisdom and abstract doctrine a man may possess from one stage of his Christian life to another. It cannot apply to the kerygma in relation to wisdom, between which the priority is transcendental rather than temporal. In other words, we cannot impose a rigid chronological straight jacket on wisdom and insist that it must always follow the hearing of the gospel as defined by human decision. The hearing of the gospel is much more a question of God's decision, and therefore less definable by a point of time. As judged by relative standards, wisdom may very well precede decision — even though, as we said, it will always be a sign of the presence of the Spirit.

A further observation which will caution us against the imposition of a rigid chronological priority is the implicitly Trinitarian character of Paul's conception of wisdom. It involves not only a wisdom imparted by the Holy Spirit, but a wisdom of the Son and of the Father. Christ crucified is, for example, among other things the wisdom of God (I Cor. 1:24), beside whom there is a wisdom integral to the purpose of the Father according to which the world by wisdom knew him not (I Cor. 1:21). Each form of this trifold wisdom is integral to the others, as we would naturally expect from the unity within the Trinity. The hidden purpose of the Father by which the world, on the basis of its own wisdom, knew him not is integral, for example, with the wisdom of the crucified one. This is why it pleased God by the foolishness of the kerygma to save them that believe (I Cor. 1:21). At the same time both of these are integral to the wisdom imparted by the Holy Spirit, as we have already implied in our emphasis on the wisdom of the Spirit as a living form of gospel insight.

The purpose of calling attention to these rich and complex dimensions of Paul's conception is chiefly to indicate that the wisdom imparted by the Holy Spirit is not a wisdom that begins *de novo* with the Spirit, but one that is anterior to it in the cross itself and anterior to the cross in the redemptive purpose of the Father. In these respects teaching, in its deeper hidden nature, is not something merely added to the gospel and to the purpose of the Father implicit in the gospel, but in some strange way integral to them. There is, for example, a kind of teaching that comes of being crucified with Christ in the hearing of faith, and there is a kind of teaching that comes of recognizing the hand of the Father in history if one has eyes to see and ears to hear. By this we do not mean three forms which follow one another, as if the wisdom of the Father and of the Son and Spirit constituted a chronological series, because this would be a denial of the contemporaneity of each. For, as we have emphasized, this contemporaneity is a vital aspect of their unity. In urging this understanding of wisdom as primarily Trinitarian and essentially a living insight which comes of the contemporaneity of the gospel, it should be said finally that it is not intended to exclude abstract doctrine, moral precepts, and propositional truth from the total concept of wisdom but that these, because they are a further stage removed, are not so characteristic of the meaning of wisdom.

6 | The Recovery of the Teaching Ministry

1. *The Need for a Critique of Religion*

One of the more important conclusions arising out of our discussion is that the teaching ministry must be seen in an ideological perspective. This is only another way of saying that it must be seen in the perspective of real life, where for practical purposes, as previously stated, real life is equated with the everyday value system. This does not mean that the ideological is ultimately definitive of real life or that it is the ultimate perspective within which the teaching ministry is to be seen. It only means that it is an inescapable consideration of any approach that takes the human and historical situation seriously.

In the light of this observation it will be commonly recognized that the ideological perspective within which the Christian faith finds itself is generally described as secularism. But what will not be commonly recognized is the possibility that secularism could have any connection with what we have been describing as vacuous religion, and within such, religion could exist in a form more dangerous to the church than its naked counterpart in contemporary society. Since religion of any kind or amount is so often regarded as essentially good, the thought of its concealing an influence as incompatible with the Christian faith as secularism is for the average churchman

patently absurd. Even the thought of secularism as the em-
bodiment of an ideology with which the Christian faith is
engaged in a genuine struggle would seem extreme, and not
at all comparable to the struggle that the church experiences
in other lands where the issues are more overt and persecution
of various kinds is common. That is to say, the difficulty for
the church in those areas of the world where it is physically
secure and socially acceptable is to realize there is any serious
struggle at all. Associated with this is the difficulty of recognizing the subtle changes in the hidden depths of the human
spirit which occur along the battle line of belief and which
are highly ominous for the destiny of church and society alike.

In contrast, however, to this general attitude is a highly
significant fact which is increasingly emphasized by competent
observers of the religious situation, particularly in America
where the surge of religious interest in recent years has
attracted so much attention. It has to do with the curious association between such religion and the secularism which, according to most interpretations, ought to be in opposition to
it.[28] The two are so often interwoven in spirit and so indistinguishable in practice that it is difficult to entertain any
other conclusion than the sociological thesis that the two de-
rive from the same source. The question, of course, is whether
this is only peculiar to America and to recent times, or whether
it is a process that has been slowly and subtly operative for
many years over a wide area in many lands, but which, due
to the effects of rapid social change, has exhibited itself in
America in a more phenomenal form. The possibility of an
affinity between religion and secularism arises from the fact
that such religion by its vacuity, by the "erosion of its particularity " and the dissolution of its tradition, including the
content of the Bible, is able to unite with anything. The evidence of its affinity for nationalism, which can result in its

transformation from a relatively quiet folk religion into a militant national religion, will illustrate what this means.

The God of vacuous religion, who is only God-in-general, and whose principal attributes, according to a recent study, are his manageableness, his coziness, and his jolly good temper, and who exists as a patron of culture and of national interests and is captive to their demands is, to say the least, not the God and Father of our Lord Jesus Christ.[29] He is a convenience whose function in the total life of the people is that of an idol and whose persuasiveness is that of an ideology. Some would go farther and assert that there is little difference between the religious allegiance to such a God and atheism, even though at first sight they seem so far apart. "A nonexistent God and a completely captive God are very much alike; under the one or the other ' all things are permissible.' "[30]

In this respect the connection between religion and secularism affords a significant parallel with that which Barth recognizes between mysticism and atheism.[31] It is significant because vacuous religion bears such a close resemblance to mysticism, and secularism to atheism, that his comments are especially pertinent to the situation under discussion. These, as they appear in his analysis of religion as unbelief, are unequivocal. " Mysticism is esoteric atheism," whereas " atheism nearly always means secularism." The main difference between them is that atheism in comparison with mysticism is artless, because " it lives on and by its negation," which means a " blabbing out of the secret " implicit in mysticism. If this analysis is correct, the surge of religion, in so far as it is vacuous, is essentially unstable and in the course of time could enter the atheistic phase with the same spontaneity that it now possesses. Or, before this happened, it could resolve itself into a syncretism of the greatest variety of ingredients, including many that by this time would have been contributed by the reinvigorated religions of the East, along with those humanisms which arise out of the educational and scientific world.

From these trends and possibilities it will be evident that more attention is required for the purpose of developing an adequate critique of religion. Not all religion is good because it is religion. "There is nothing in the Bible to support the view that religion is necessarily a good thing. Scripture has no ax to grind for religion; on the contrary it is highly suspicious of much that passes for religion." [32] Of this fact no better confirmation could be found than the role of religion in putting Christ to death. Consistent with it is the further fact that in comparison with the opposition to the gospel which comes of irreligion, the sharpest opposition frequently comes of religion and its quasi-religious ideological substitutes. As if to emphasize the point, and notwithstanding Bonhoeffer's penetrating observations of a religionless world which in another sense confirm the necessity of a critique of religion, a noted student of world religions is constrained to say: "The modern world is in fact the most prolific producer of new religions, cults, pseudo religions, and idolatries that ever was, demonstrating thereby that man has an ineradicable religious appetite." [33] Consequently it is not too much to say that one of the major problems of all forms of Christian education is what to do with religion. At the level of theological education, the necessity of a thorough grasp of world religions and particularly of the ideological perspective would seem to be essential, not only for a better knowledge of the contemporary situation but for a better understanding of the distinctiveness of the Christian faith.

The need for a critique of religion is particularly emphatic because of the frequent assumption that religion and Biblical faith are in their essential nature supplementary, and that it is possible to proceed from the one to the other as if from a lower to a higher stage of education. Religion in this respect has been compared to a lower stage, whereas Biblical faith has been compared to a higher stage, with religion fulfilling the role of a schoolmaster whose task has been interpreted as leading the learner to Christ.

But alongside of this assumption, paralleling it after the fashion of a strong competitor, is an opposite assumption which operates on the same premise of the supplementary nature of religion and Biblical faith. According to it, Biblical faith is the lower stage whereas religion is the higher, where the higher is conceived as an advance beyond the particularity that characterizes Biblical faith. In such a reversal of the assumption, religious vacuity is transformed into a supreme virtue and becomes the goal of religious development. All particularity is to be left behind as if only a childish fancy to be forgotten with increased maturity. All concern for the identity of God, his action in history, his will as revealed so that many can speak of being claimed and commissioned by him, is to be wiped out with one stroke as a lower, primitive stage which is only of a temporary significance in the development of religion.[34]

2. The Development of Discrimination

A second conclusion, and one cognate to a critique of religion in the ideological perspective, is that there is a need for the teaching ministry to concentrate upon the development of the ability to discriminate. This means an emphasis upon the recognition of significant differences as a major objective of the educational program, particularly at the adult and adolescent level. To a considerable extent it means a reorientation with respect to the necessity of thinking, which we have already distinguished from the Socratic tradition and qualified in its relational character as a confrontation of the learner by the transcendental differential with its implicit offense. As such it should not be confused with the desire to indoctrinate or to preserve certain historic differences for sentimental and prejudicial reasons, including much that belongs to the particularity of the Christian faith. The primary purpose cannot be one of preservation, because this could hardly be other than a desire to maintain the security of the institutional church at the expense of the word of God — a desire always determined by fear and the idea of defense. Instead, the purpose is that of bringing Christian particularity forth from its tomb, of loosing it from its grave clothes and letting it free so that it might confront the learner with its rich and decisive possibilities as suggested by the educational implications of the conversations of Jesus. This, it would seem, is the only form of particularity that would be other than a liability to the church in the ideological struggle.

The necessity of such an emphasis should hardly be considered as other than elemental — as the first concern of every Christian in order to understand his faith and to be a good soldier of Jesus Christ. It is by no means academic, but that practical understanding which from the point of view of any modern ideology would be expected of its followers for the purpose of maintaining its identity, propagating its beliefs, and engaging in the inevitable conflict which arises out of such activity. Surely the average Christian should be able to understand that two religions worshiping God are not necessarily worshiping the same God because the same name is applied to both, nor engaging in the same activity because the same word " prayer " describes it. Similarly with holiness and sin, spirit and flesh, and other categories — the same word used of each, whatever the language, is no proof the same thing is meant. Unless this is thoroughly appreciated, words will only conceal rather than reveal meaning and will become an obstacle to thought rather than an aid, both in the theological class-room and in the village pulpit. If, on the contrary, words are regularly sharpened in meaning as the blade of a cutting in-strument is sharpened, they will perform their proper function to a surprising extent. The particularization of meaning will develop the discrimination of the learner and acquaint him better with the terminology of the faith he professes, which in a secular field would be a basic requirement. This, as an initial objective, would seem to be highly important at all levels of the teaching ministry and especially at the level of the local congregation, where the terminology of the Bible and of the Christian faith is so often used but so seldom explained. What can be done at this level to make familiar terms and titles more meaningful to the average worshiper is a most in-teresting possibility which should fascinate the resourceful minister.

But the scope of discrimination reaches beyond the termi-nology of faith — beyond the key words and the distinctive meaning of each. It comprehends each book of the Bible and the Bible as a whole, and this in relation to real life both in the ancient past and in the modern world. This was implied in our conception of relational hermeneutics which was mainly illustrated from the book of The Acts. What was done with the book of The Acts can be done to a greater or lesser extent with the whole Bible, allowing for minor modifications. It can be in-terpreted and taught with an eye to the relational which is a form of thinking inevitable in any ideological situation. To be more specific, it should be possible to develop what might be called a boundary-line curriculum as a supplement to a subject-matter curriculum — using the term "curriculum" for the moment quite broadly as any selection for pulpit or class-room purposes. A boundary line would have reference to any historical line of difference involving tension and conflict with an ideological connotation, and particularly one that at the same time concealed a transcendental differential. In a sense it might be regarded as a problem curriculum with the meaning of problem focused in the manner already indicated, which has as its purpose a better understanding of the significance of the Bible in the present perspective. The assumption is that the better the interpreter can rediscover the original lines of ideological conflict, particularly those in the midst of which or against which the Word of God was heard, the better the Bible can be used in the present situation. It is upon this background, moreover, that the previous reference to the sharpening of words can be better understood.

In suggesting the possibility of such a curriculum, it ought not to be supposed that the main idea is that of taking the lessons of one period of history and applying them to another. The familiar idea of " applied " knowledge which would presuppose a subject-matter curriculum would also presuppose a quantum conception of truth, and this would only vitiate what we mean by relational thinking. The truth in this respect is not something static which is " applied " to a situation in a mechanical manner. By such a procedure nothing further could be learned of the truth than was already learned in the discovery. The communication of truth would not be seen as an equally important means of learning more of the same truth. The metaphor of " application," with its implied metaphor of the " transportation " of packaged truth from one situation to another, is a failure to recognize that communication is a living, creative process in which new aspects of the truth are always emerging. The hidden as well as unprecedented factors in any situation only serve to underline this point. In the life-and-death struggle of faith with unbelief it is not difficult to see which conception of truth and communication has the advantage.

There is a further reason why we cannot speak of taking the lessons of one period of history and applying them to another. It concerns the fact that the nearer the teacher comes to the transcendental differential in attempting to deal with a typical boundary-line problem, the nearer he comes to a form of truth that cannot be taught. At this point the directness of teaching is limited by the indirectness of revelation. At this point teaching is transposed into preaching, because preaching by its nature stands nearer to revelation. Instead now, as in teaching where the movement is from ignorance to knowledge, the movement is from knowledge to ignorance — not of course to the original ignorance of directness, but to a new ignorance, the ignorance of indirectness, which is characterized by the fact that it is capable of bowing in wonder and amazement before God. Similarly with the offense — the offense mediated by teaching, which is the offense of directness and therefore of judgment, is transposed into the offense mediated by preaching, which is the offense of indirectness and therefore of mercy. Such indirectness cannot be " applied." Revelation and the ignorance of indirectness which comes of it cannot be taken from one situation and applied as a lesson to another. On this matter two further observations should be made. First, it cannot be emphasized enough how closely preaching and teaching are unified, and how the teaching of a boundary-line problem will of necessity be transposed into preaching.[35] Similarly with the two forms of offense — it cannot be emphasized enough that the offense of judgment is always mysteriously related to the offense of mercy. The other observation concerns the importance of indirectness and therefore of genuine preaching in any ideological situation. Such preaching always engages in the struggle from behind, from the inside — from any direction except the one that permits the opponent to use the strategy of directness. It fights him with forgiveness. It fights for him even though it has to fight against his idol. It conquers from within.

In looking back on the whole suggestion of a boundary-line curriculum, it should not be supposed that the emphasis on significant differences will dull the sensitivity to important similarities. The important thing to remember is the impossibility of picking out differences without implicitly defining their opposites (similarities). On this basis there is a greater likelihood of the Christian's learning, not only how he differs from his ideological opponent, but what he has in common with him. The weakness in so far as faith has been affected by vacuous religion is just the opposite — its almost total lack of awareness. It has no idea of the legitimate differences that separate it from opposing ideologies or of the legitimate things it has in common with them. As a result, when such faith chooses to fight it fights blindly, because it has no power of discrimination derivative of the Word of God. But when it does possess such power it has several advantages. It has a foil against the indiscriminate attitude that all gods are the same and that all worshipers are going to the same place. It has a protection against the tactics of infiltration by which the ideological attempts to identify itself with faith, and most significantly a stimulant for creative thinking within itself which is its finest strategy.

3. The Question of Motivation

The protests which from a motivational point of view will be offered by various theories of learning against the conception of teaching we have developed and especially against the offense of the truth mediated by it are only to be expected. It will be urged, for example, that such a conception would dampen all enthusiasm for learning, that it would even turn the learner against the Bible and the faith and perhaps even contribute to an excessively serious and possibly unhealthy attitude to life. Questions will be raised about its place in the classroom, where it is difficult enough already to foster a favorable atmosphere for learning, and about its place in the pulpit, from which the burdened listener naturally expects a message of comfort. Altogether it will be regarded as so contradictory of normal motivation that its pedagogical status will be suspect.

The difficulty in evaluating these protests is that they all involve a measure of truth and cannot be dismissed as groundless. Admittedly there is a certain contradiction of normal motivation, as the discussion on the offense of the teaching ministry should plainly indicate (Ch. 2). The teacher will always have to contend with the possibility that members of his church or class, apart from justifiable personal reasons, may react negatively to the offense of the Bible and turn away like those disciples who at a certain stage in the ministry of Christ went back and walked no more with him (John 6:66). This possibility is evident all through the New Testament. Some follow Christ to learn more of him and of his teaching, but they soon abandon him at the thought of discipleship. They have not counted the cost. Others who have followed him are eventually scandalized, so that among his closest disciples one one finally denies him and another betrays him. That the same problem should be reflected in the teaching ministry is no surprise.

On the other hand, the presupposition that it introduces into the learning situation an offensiveness of a social nature to which the response of the learner is consistently negative is highly questionable. No teacher is able to provide the offense according to plan and manipulate it for the purposes of motivation. The offense mediated by the teaching ministry is not of this nature, even if it has been described as the offense of directness and equivalent to judgment. It is never at the disposal of the teacher. It pertains rather to that dimension of Biblical truth which is strange, absurd, and costly, and provocative of wonder in children and adults alike. Children perhaps may understand it at times better than adults. Above all, it ought not to be dismissed as a form of authoritarianism, because the quality of suffering that it involves is not the product of any kind of coercion. Even if it be emphasized that the offense is derivative of the transcendental, it would be wrong to think of the transcendental after the analogy of human coercion. The suffering instead is indigenous to the truth it involves. This is why in a surprising number of cases the learner, instead of recoiling from it, is profoundly attracted by it, as the New Testament suggests in respect to the nailing of Christ to the cross: " And I, if I be lifted up . . . , will draw all men unto me." It possesses a strange fascination which lays hold upon the learner, even if at the same time it repels him. Under these circumstances he will be led to accept the suffering willingly, not out of a morbid satisfaction suggestive of a self-punitive tendency, but out of a recognition of its inherent validity. Even in the secular sense, what stands over against the learner as different, as difficult and dangerous, often fascinates and challenges and sometimes wins him. Always there is a serious risk in any kind of learning that the easier we make things for the learner the more he will despise us for it in the end. The church has made too many unnecessary enemies for itself by the easy standards that have often obtained in all branches of its teaching ministry not to consider this risk.

Accordingly it is the responsibility of the teacher to present the truth of the Bible with such honesty and thoroughness that its meaning will be recognized to the fullest extent. He will not relieve the learner of difficulty by resorting to irresponsible forms of simplification which only distort the meaning for him. Even with those forms of simplification which are responsible and therefore legitimate pedagogy, the point may be reached where the learner is allowed to go his way with no solution for the various problems as he formulated them. A classic, although by no means isolated, example of this is Christ's refusal to adjust his truth to the rich young ruler, who went sorrowfully away because he could not accept the conditions of discipleship. With all that can be said of Christ's masterful simplification of truth in his parables and sayings, his intention was never that of adjusting it to men but rather, them to it. For the same reason he never argued with the religious authorities of his day on the same terms as they argued with one another. At no time did he sacrifice his distinctiveness for the sake of agreement.

The primary emphasis in motivation, as far as the Christian teacher is concerned, is therefore not that of beginning with the needs of the individual. These are important, of course, in so far as they are the elemental needs definitive of his humanity, but as such they are best served by making them, not ends in themselves, but of service to the truth that is in Christ. A somewhat indiscriminate emphasis on needs is always confronted by the fact that in actuality they are as numerous as the voices in secular society clamoring for the individual's attention and money. "Needs are looked upon today as if they were holy, as if they contained the totality of existence. Needs are our gods and we toil and spare no effort to gratify them. . . . Short is the way from need to greed." It is the same with the multitudinous interests that have been inculcated into the individual and with which the teacher is tempted to begin without careful discrimination. They soon determine everything and limit the possibility of what he will learn. In this respect the remark is appropiate: " Interest is a subjective, dividing

principle. . . . It is just because the power of interest is tyran-
nizing our lives, determining our views and action, that we
lose sight of the values that count most." [36]

The least that can be said is that the teacher ought to be
cautious about the accepted principle of motivation which appeals to the needs and interests of the individual in the communication of truth. Needs and interests are always to a large
extent ideologically conditioned. They are built into the individual by secular society, whose influence is mediated by the
home, school, and community. One important reason for recognizing the context out of which such needs and interests
arise is that it provides a corrective for the erroneous optimism
that Christ is the solution for every problem and the answer
to every question. As suggested by his treatment of the rich
young ruler, the opposite is frequently true. The needs and interests which are rooted in the secular soil and which in luxu-
riant fashion sprout problems and questions until the tangled
overgrowth chokes out everything else often have to be dug
up. The gardener has to use his spade and his pruning knife,
which as his solution and answer is of a much different character (John 15:2). Therefore it has to be asserted that a Christ
who could answer all the questions that curious people brought
to him would be transformed into an oracle at the disposal of
men. Like every other oracle, he would operate on the basis of
a power that presumed to see into specific situations and into
the future with clairvoyant skill which would be expressive of
the pagan conception of direct revelation. But the Christ of
the New Testament is not an oracle, as is evident from those
occasions on which people tried to question him. He is not at
the disposal of the " needs " and " interests " out of which
these questions arise and which for the most part are ideologically conditioned. Instead, it is he who puts the questions. It
is he who interrogates. " Come unto me, all ye that labor and

are heavy laden, and I will give you the rest." (Matt. 11:28.) "For what shall it profit a man, if he shall gain the whole world, and lose his own soul?" (Mark 8:36.) What oracle ever talked this way?

4. The Implicit Difficulty of Teaching

If the present study of the teaching ministry has succeeded in creating the impression to some degree that such a ministry is difficult, it will have achieved one of its principal purposes. Considering the orgy of easy faith and cheap grace, our responsibility is not to make the teaching ministry still easier, but to make it more difficult in the hope of stimulating greater diligence and higher standards at every level. This is surely justifiable in the light of those burdens of mind and spirit from which no prophet or apostle was ever known to spare the people of God when life-and-death issues confronted them. It should not be expected therefore that the conception of teaching that has emerged from our discussion will be readily applicable to the Sunday school and to the weekly requirements of the pulpit. It is not intended as a panacea or as a promotional device for quick success. It is rather an attempt to reflect upon the nature and the responsibility of the teaching ministry in a world that is rapidly changing, that is charged with terrifying possibilities, and that offers the church no respite from deep, inexorable conflict of faith, thought, and life. Certainly the teaching ministry is difficult. So is the preaching ministry. So is the Christian life. Undoubtedly there are forms of teaching that are easier than others — the telling of a story, the communication of facts — but these do not represent the genius of teaching either in the best secular or Christian sense. They are necessary because they provide the form and substance of teaching, but they do not constitute its life and spirit. Unless touched by the quickening power of a mas-

ter, they will remain as dead as dust. Real teaching is always
creative and therefore able to make the old become new and
equally able to prevent the new from becoming novel. And
this means that it honors the intelligible and the power of
thinking in its highest form, where thinking has not become
an end in itself as always tends to happen in intellectualism,
but where it seeks only to serve the truth and to serve it in
the name of Him who is the truth.

Teaching is always more difficult when the learner is active
and encouraged to think, because under these circumstances
at their best the creative impulse of one mind meets that of
another, with the possibility that at the point where both are
confronted with the word that cannot be taught it may be
said by one of the other " deep calleth unto deep." In such
thought which is at the same time the derivative of the heart,
which is the motivational origin of the learner's life, the teacher
will be confronted with the learner's secret. Only on rare occasions will the teacher catch a glimpse of this secret. Always it
is easier to open and read a book than a learner, because the
price of such an achievement, both for the learner and the
teacher, is the price of integrity — that truth of the inward
part which substantiates the truth of the mind.

But it is no easier for the teacher to find the secret of the
age than of the individual, because the battle line of the spirit
in any society or civilization is submerged. It is almost always
unacknowledged. Except for this the ideological struggle in
any instance would not have penetrated so deeply. In so far
as the same spirit has penetrated the church, the battle line of
faith and unbelief will also remain submerged and unacknowledged. Victory will not be won by agreement on what beliefs
and practices are held in common (unity) or by a cordial recognition of those which divide. These may be achieved without touching the sensitive boundary line where faith meets op-

position and is engaged in struggle — where the hidden battle of the age is being waged for the possession of the mind and spirit and eventually for the whole man.

Consequently the teacher should not expect too much, or be carried away with the thought of his ability to reform the church, because this would betray the spirit of a novice, not of one who has counted the cost. The most that can be expected is that here and there, in some places more than others, and always in unexpected places, both high and low, a few will have grasped the real reason why teaching is difficult. This is not pessimism but the recognition that the church, like Israel of old, is at all times quickened by its suffering remnant.

⇌ Notes

1. S. W. Blizzard, " The Minister's Dilemma," *The Christian Century,* April 25, 1956; " The Protestant Parish Minister's Integrating Roles," *Religious Education,* July-Aug., 1958; " The Parish Minister's Self Image of His Master Role," *Pastoral Psychology,* Dec., 1958.

2. *Re-Study of Religious Education, Presbyterian Church in the U.S.,* p. 48. Directed by Lewis J. Sherrill. John Knox Press, 1948.

3. Qualifications of the average Sunday school teacher in note 2, above, p. 63.

4. On the ministry and theological education see: Niebuhr, Williams, Gustafson, *The Advancement of Theological Education* (Harper & Brothers, 1957); Niebuhr and Williams, *The Ministry in Historical Perspectives* (Harper & Brothers, 1956).

5. Jerald C. Brauer, " Protestant Theological Education," *The Christian Century,* April 25, 1956. Article illustrates how religious experience has been emphasized at the expense of truth.

6. W. A. Curtis, *Jesus Christ the Teacher.* Oxford University Press, London, 1943. Author is sensitive to the problem of the subordination of the teaching ministry. See Ch. 1, p. 20. Antiintellectualism should not be overlooked as a contributory factor

to the subordination of the teaching ministry. See, for example, R. Fulop-Miller, "The New Revolt Against Reason," *Hibbert Journal* 34 (1935–1936), 178–193; J. R. Whatmough, "Anti-Intellectualism," *Hibbert Journal* 56 (1958), 352–360.

7. *Kerygma and Myth,* ed. by H. W. Bartsch, tr. by R. H. Fuller. (S.P.C.K., London, 1953). See especially Bultmann's essay, pp. 1–44.

8. Hendrik Kraemer, *The Communication of the Christian Faith* (The Westminster Press, 1956), p. 93.

9. Dietrich Bonhoeffer, "God in an Irreligious World," *Ecumenical Review,* 4 (1951–1952), 131–138.

10. Joseph Haroutunian, "How to Hear the Gospel," Centenary Address, Knox College, Toronto, 1958.

11. On the role of the teacher, see the following: K. H. Rengstorf, article on "*Didasko, Didaskalos, Didaskalia, Didache,*" in Kittel's *Theologisches Wörterbuch zum Neuen Testament,* II, 138–167 (Stuttgart, 1935); C. H. Dodd, "Jesus as Teacher and Prophet," Ch. 3 in *Mysterium Christi,* ed. by Bell and Deissmann (Longmans, Green & Co., Ltd., London, 1930); Floyd V. Filson, "The Christian Teacher in the First Century," *Journal of Biblical Literature* 60 (1941), 317–328; B. C. Dilz, "Christ and the Curriculum," Ch. 4 in *The Sense of Wonder* (McClelland & Stewart, Ltd., Toronto, 1953).

The conception of thinking set forth in Ch. 2 of this book is developed further in Ch. 4, "Relational Hermeneutics."

12. See Karl Barth on the simplicity of God, *Church Dogmatics,* 2, Pt. 1, 445–461 (T. & T. Clark, Edinburgh, 1957).

13. Based on lines from T. S. Eliot, Choruses from "The Rock,"

in *Collected Poems 1909–1935* (Faber and Faber, Ltd., London, 1951), p. 157.

14. Will Herberg, *Protestant, Catholic, Jew*. Doubleday & Co., Inc., 1955.

15. See Arnold Toynbee, *An Historian's Approach to Religion*. Oxford University Press, London, 1956.

16. A. Roy Eckardt, *The Surge of Piety in America*. Association Press, 1958. See description of folk religion, Ch. 2. See also Martin Marty, *The New Shape of American Religion*. Harper & Brothers, 1958.

17. Rudolf Bultmann, *Essays: Philosophical and Theological* (S.C.M. Press, Ltd., London, 1955). See "Problem of Hermeneutics," pp. 234–261.

18. For present purposes, literalism may be defined as that conception of the text which assumes that its essential meaning can be read off directly. This, strictly speaking, fails to allow for the testimony of the Holy Spirit, ignores the context, and recognizes little or no place for a teacher. To regard it as untenable does not relieve one, however, from submitting to the discipline of the text or from the responsibility of establishing its fullest and most accurate meaning.

19. J. N. Sanders, "The Problem of Exegesis," *Theology*, 43 (1941), 324–332. I am indebted to this article for its emphasis on the importance of the ideological.

20. W. O. E. Oesterley, *The Gospel Parables in the Light of Their Jewish Background* (S.P.C.K., London, 1936), p. 162.

21. This conception is best illustrated by C. H. Dodd, whose

earlier publication *Apostolic Preaching and Its Developments* pioneered it, at least in the English-speaking world.

22. Consider the emphasis on the proclamation of the "facts" found in E. F. Scott, *Varieties of Religion in the New Testament* (Charles Scribner's Sons, 1944), pp. 22–23.

23. E. C. Hoskyns, *The Fourth Gospel,* Vol. 1, ed. by F. N. Davey, (S.P.C.K., London, 1943). See introductory essays on the historical and theological tension in this Gospel as an interpretation of the unity here implied.

24. W. Baird, "What Is the Kerygma?" *Journal of Biblical Literature* 76 (1957), 181–191.

25. J. Jeremias, *The Parables of Jesus* (Charles Scribner's Sons, 1955). See especially Ch. 3, "The Message of the Parables of Jesus."

26. J. J. Vincent, "Didactic Kerygma in the Synoptic Gospels," *Scottish Journal of Theology* (Sept., 1957), 262–273.

27. William Manson, *Jesus the Messiah* (Hodder & Stoughton, Ltd., London, 1943), pp. 54–55. See also Chs. 4 and 5.

28. On the association of religion with secularism, see: Will Herberg, *op. cit.;* Martin Marty, *op. cit.*

29. Martin Marty, *op. cit.*

30. *Ibid.,* p. 40.

31. Karl Barth, *Church Dogmatics,* 1, Pt. 3, 318–325.

32. A. Roy Eckardt, "The New Look in American Piety," *The Christian Century,* Nov. 17, 1954.

33. Hendrik Kraemer, *op. cit.,* p. 103.

34. Erich Fromm, *The Art of Loving* (Harper & Brothers, 1956). See pp. 69–70 as an illustration of this point of view.

35. Karl Barth, *Church Dogmatics,* 4, Pt. 2, p. 200. The writer favors a more closely integrated conception of teaching (*didachē*) and authority (*eksousia*) than indicated in this excellent treatment.

36. A. J. Herschel, "The Religious Message," an essay in *Religion in America,* ed. by J. Cogley (Meridian Books, Inc., 1958), pp. 247–249.